SQL for Beginners

A Step-by-Step Guide to Learn SQL (Structured Query Language) From Installation to Database Management and Database Administration

Julian James McKinnon

Table of Contents

Introduction	**8**
How to Start Coding	11
Chapter 1: Database Changes	**18**
Databases	21
Chapter 2: Basic Background of SQL	**41**
What Is SQL?	42
How This Works With Your Database	45
Why Is SQL So Great?	46
Working on the Databases	50
Chapter 3: Installation	**57**
Installing Oracle Database	58
Installing the SQL Developer	62

Using the SQL Developer ... 67

How to Create a Database Connection ... 68

How to Import or Export Database Connection ... 70

Creating a MySQL Database ... 71

Chapter 4: Data Types — 76

Access Data Types ... 76

MySQL Data Types ... 78

Oracle Data Types ... 83

SQL Server ... 87

Chapter 5: Types of Symbols Used — 93

SQL symbols ... 93

Chapter 6: SQL Triggers — 96

Trigger Syntax ... 97

Chapter 7: Using VIEWS in SQL — 105

How to Create VIEWS ... 107

Using the Keyword WITH CHECK OPTION ... 110

Chapter 8: Using Operators to Categorize Information ... 115

Logical Operators ... 116

Comparison Operators ... 117

Arithmetic Operations ... 119

Operators to Use When Negating Conditions ... 121

Conjunctive Operators ... 122

Chapter 9: Users and Roles ... 124

Logins to the Server ... 124

Assigning Roles in the Database ... 126

Commands to Help With Users and Roles ... 129

Chapter 10: Normalizing Your Database ... 132

How Do I Normalize the Database? ... 133

Chapter 11: The Security of Databases ... 145

Microsoft's Fixed Server Roles ... 150

TOP Clause   152

Chapter 12: Summary of Database Development   **155**

The Components of a Database   155

The Lifecycle of System Development   158

How to Create a Table   163

How to Delete Tables   164

Checking the Integrity of a Database   166

Chapter 13: Database Administration   **168**

Setting up a Maintenance Plan in SQL Server   172

Running the Maintenance Plan   178

Backup and Recovery   182

Chapter 14: Real-World Uses   **191**

Conclusion   **199**

It Is All About Asking Good Questions   200

Choosing the Right Database Occupation   201

© **Copyright 2020 - All rights reserved.**
The content contained within this book may not be reproduced, duplicated or transmitted without direct written permission from the author or the publisher.
Under no circumstances will any blame or legal responsibility be held against the publisher, or author, for any damages, reparation, or monetary loss due to the information contained within this book. Either directly or indirectly.

Legal Notice:
This book is copyright protected. This book is only for personal use. You cannot amend, distribute, sell, use, quote or paraphrase any part, or the content within this book, without the consent of the author or publisher.

Disclaimer Notice:
Please note the information contained within this document is for educational and entertainment purposes only. All effort has been executed to present accurate, up to date, and reliable, complete information. No warranties of any kind are declared or implied. Readers acknowledge that the author is not engaging in the rendering of legal, financial, medical or professional advice. The content within this book has been derived from various sources. Please consult a licensed professional before attempting any techniques outlined in this book.
By reading this document, the reader agrees that under no circumstances is the author responsible for any losses, direct or indirect, which are incurred as a result of the use of the information contained within this document, including, but not limited to, — errors, omissions, or inaccuracies.

Introduction

Network programs are larger and more flexible. In many cases, the fundamental scheme of operations is mainly a mix of scripts that handle the command of a database.

Besides the variety of languages and pre-existing sources, the method to "talk" between one another may usually be challenging and complicated, fortunately for us, the presence of the requirements that permit us to do the typical methods by way of a widespread form can make this particular perplexing task even more simple.

That is what Structured Query Language (SQL) is based on, which typically is only a worldwide common language of interaction within databases. That is precisely why, the Structured Query Language (SQL) is a standardized language that allows most people to apply some language e.g. PHP or ASP, in conjunction with any particular database e.g. MySQL, MS Access, SQL Server.

If you are interested in learning a new coding language, there are a lot of different options that you can choose from, and it depends on what you are looking for and what you want to do with them.

Some of these languages are good for helping you to create a good website. Some are good for creating a smartphone application or for working on your own game to share with others.

And then you can also choose a coding language that is like SQL, which is meant to help businesses stay organized and keep track of their information without all the challenges that can come with this.

Traditionally, many companies would choose to work with the "Database Management System," or the DBMS to help them to keep organized and to keep track of their customers and their products.

This was the first option that was on the market for this kind of organization, and it does work well. Some newer methods have changed the way that companies can sort and hold their information.

Even when it comes to the most basic management system for data that you can choose, you will see that there is a ton more power and security than you would have found in the past.

Big companies will be responsible for holding onto a lot of data, and some of this data will include personal information about their customers like addresses, names, and credit card information.

Because of the more complex sort of information that these businesses need to store, a new "Relational Database Management System" has been created to help keep this information safe in a way that the DBMS has not been able to.

Now, as a business owner, there are some different options that you can pick from when you want to get a good database management system.

Most business owners like to go with SQL because it is one of the best options out there.

The SQL language is easy to use, was designed to work well with businesses, and will give you all the tools that you need to make sure that your information is safe.

Let's take some more time to look at this SQL and learn how to make it work for your business.

How to Start Coding

SQL is easy to learn, and you won't have a lot of different commands to bring up the information that you want.

In this chapter, we are going to spend some time learning some of these commands as well as separating the commands into the 6 different categories that are the best for them.

These 6 categories include:

Data Definition Language

This one is also known as the DDL, and it is one of the aspects that is inside of your SQL program that is in charge of allowing you to generate objects into the database before arranging them the way that you enjoy the best.

For example, this is the aspect of the system that you will use when you would like to make changes, such as adding or deleting objects, out of the table.

The commands that you would be able to use for this include:

- Drop index
- Drop view

- Create an index
- Alter index
- Alter table
- Drop table
- Create a table

Data Query Language

When you are working in DQL (Data Query Language), you are working with what many consider a really powerful aspect of what they can do with SQL, especially when you are working on a database system that is considered more modern.

There is just one command that is needed to work with the DQL part, and this command is the "Select" command.

You can use this command in various ways including using it to run queries when you are inside of a relational database.

If you were interested in getting more detailed results, you would need to use the Select command through DQL to make this happen.

Data Control Language

The DCL (Data Control Language) is another component of SQL that you should learn to use, and it is the commands that the user works with any time that they want to control who is allowed to get on the database.

If you are dealing with personal information like credit card information, it is a good idea to have some limitations on who can get onto the system and get the information.

This DCL command is used to help generate the objects that are related to who can access the information in the database, including who will be able to distribute the information.

There are a few commands that are helpful when you are working on DCL including:

- Create synonym
- Grand
- Alter password
- Revoke

Data Administration Commands

When it comes to some of the commands that you can use inside SQL, you can also use them to audit or analyze the operation that is inside of the database.

They are also good to assess the performance of the database overall with the help of some of these commands.

If you would like to fix something that is causing issues on the system or you would like to get rid of some of the bugs on the system, these are the commands that you are going to need to work with.

While there are some options that you can choose from with these commands, the 2 most popular options include:

- Stop audit
- Start audit

One of the things that you need to remember when working with SQL is that data administration and database administration are going to be 2 different ideas inside the system.

For example, database administration is going to be the part that will manage all your databases, including the different commands that you are setting up in SQL and they will also be more specific to the implementation that is done in SQL.

Transactional Control Commands

If you are trying to manage and keep track of some of the transactions that are going on with your database with you and the customer, the transactional control commands are the right ones to use.

If you are a company that uses its website to sell products online, the transactional control commands are going to help make sure that you can keep all of this inline.

There are several things that you will be able to use these transactional control commands for, including:

Commit

This is the command that you will need to use to save information that relates to the different transactions that are inside your database.

Savepoint

This is the command that you will be able to use to generate different points inside the group of transactions.

This is also the one that you can use at the same time as the Rollback Command.

Rollback

This command is the one that you will use whenever you are looking through the database, and you would like to undo at least one of the transactions inside.

Set Transaction

This command is the one that you can use any time that you are trying to take the transactions in your database and give them names.

You will often use this one whenever you are trying to label things for a bit more organization.

All 6 of these types are going to be important based on the results that you would like to get out of your search.

Each of these will be explored a bit more as we go through this guidebook so that you understand better how to use them, when to use them, and how to divide up the information in the proper way to avoid issues and to keep your database nice and organized with the help of the SQL language.

Each company that provides database products has its path to be an "expert."

For instance, Microsoft offers an assortment of accreditation to guarantee that each Microsoft SQL Certified meets their criteria.

Oracle does the same thing with its Certification process.

Chapter 1: Database Changes

Computers have, without a doubt, revolutionized every task we perform. We no longer rely on typewriters to record text documents, or mechanical calculators to perform arithmetic calculations for us.

Furthermore, we no longer have to rely on entire rooms and basements filled with cabinets packed to the brim with folders and files. Storing information is no longer a question of physical space.

Computers are capable of a lot more when compared to the old techniques and tools, they are faster, and they barely require any space.

However, there are downsides that we need to take into consideration as well. For instance, we no longer physically access all the information we store.

When a hard drive fails or a computer crashes, a specialized technician is the only hope, and recovering lost data can take time. Even then, there's no guarantee that all of the data is intact.

On the other hand, papers didn't give you errors. The worst scenario involved spilling coffee on a copy or dropping it and picking it up.

Modern data storage requires several precautions to keep the data safe from a computer, as well as human failures.

Here are the main factors you need to take into consideration when storing information:

- The process of storing data needs to be fast because it needs to be performed often.
- Reliable storage is crucial. You need to make sure the data will still be there after years of storage.
- Losing it in the far reaches of cyberspace because of unreliable service or faulty hardware can cause expensive damages.
- Retrieving data needs to be fast and as painless as possible, no matter how vast the amount of information is.
- The ability to find and extract only the information you need from the storage system is important.
- When you handle terabytes' worth of data, you need a reliable method of filtering it.

This is what databases are for. The basic principle of storing information is that if you need to manage more than 12 items of data, you should be using a database.

This is where SQL comes in. Pronounced by reading the individual letters or as the word "sequel" (there's still a debate on this among SQL specialists), SQL allows you to create a database where you can store many items and manage them.

It was created in the 70s by IBM, but even today, SQL remains a standard in the industry.

Several database types handle data management in different ways; however, we are going to deal with object-relational databases.

In the early years of SQL's development, its focus was on relational databases; however, nowadays, it relies on a hybrid model.

In this chapter, we are going to take a look at all of these notions to give you a basic understanding of SQL.

Before we dive into the technicalities, however, you should learn about databases in general, including the major models such as the relational model, and their main features.

Databases

The meaning behind the word "database" has changed so much in the past couple of decades that it barely preserves its definition.

To some people, a database refers to any number of data items contained in a book or list. To others, it refers to a repository of structured data or records, which can be accessed through a computer system.

We will focus on the second definition, which also includes SQL. Keep in mind that in this case, a record refers to the representation of an item. For instance, you are running your own business, and therefore, you will create one record for every unique client.

These records will contain several characteristics that describe the object. For example, you can include data such as names, phone numbers, addresses, and so on.

A database, however, doesn't contain only data. It also includes metadata, which has the purpose of defining the information's structure inside the database.

Why is this important? Because if you know how the data is organized, then you can access it, manage it, maintain it, and modify it.

All of this means that a database is self-describing, as it contains information on the connections between the data objects.

The metadata is reserved inside what's known as a data dictionary. The dictionary is what describes the components of a database, namely the table, the rows, columns, and so on.

On a side note, you should know that flat-file systems do not contain metadata.

This means that the programs that handle these files need to have some form of an equivalent integrated. We will discuss flat files in more detail soon.

The size of a database varies as well, depending on the number of records it contains. For instance, you can have anywhere between a dozen data objects and millions.

For now, you don't have to worry about any such limitations. However, databases can be categorized in 3 different ways:

- **Personal databases are the smallest.** They are stored on the user's personal computer and are characterized by a basic data structure.
- **Group databases, on the other hand, are more complex.** They are intended to be used by a department or team, which means that they contain a great deal more data than a personal database. This means that they also need to be accessed from multiple devices at the same time.
- **Finally, we have the enterprise version of a database.** They are huge, complex, and need the most reliable equipment to be safely stored and maintained.

As you can see, you can categorize a database by looking at 3 attributes: how large it is, how many people need to have access to it, and what kind of technical equipment it requires.

Database Management Systems

To manage a database and any applications that have access to it, we need to use a database management system. Keep in mind that a database is nothing more than a structure designed to contain information.

We need a tool that actually creates that structure and then allows us to access, maintain, or modify the data inside it. There are many such programs available for free or at a certain cost. Not all data management systems are created equally, however.

The one you need depends on your goal and requirements. For instance, some of these programs are designed to operate on professional, enterprise-grade equipment and handle massive databases.

On the other hand, some of them are intended to work on basic, personal use laptops. However, keep in mind that these tools sometimes need to function at the same time on different hardware settings running different operating systems.

Furthermore, we also have the cloud to consider as a storage option. Nowadays, you can gain public online storage through services offered by organizations such as Amazon and Microsoft. The cloud is one of those terms you will often hear in any tech field due to the massive increase in computer processing power and storage capabilities that many businesses require today.

What you should know for now in case you don't, is that the cloud is an assembly of computers that make their resources available to anyone via the Internet.

This means that anyone can access these services from the comfort of their home instead of physically connecting to a data center. In this case, a data management system with cloud capabilities can provide you with the functionality you need to manage your databases remotely.

Database management systems ensure the flow of data between the user and the system is always the same no matter the type of system and the size of the database.

Flat Files

A flat file is the most basic type of file you can work with. It is appropriately named because its data structure is minimalistic, and it only contains a list of records. Keep in mind that it doesn't contain any metadata.

With that in mind, here's an example of information kept with this type of file:

John Watson Rd	3453 S. Cabin Lane Anaheim	
Mike Moriarty Ana	6748 S. Rose Lane	Santa
Philip Baggins Aberdeen	234 Wordsworth Avenue	

Samuel Smith Street	2456 Smith Birmingham
George Took Close	543 Newton Canterbury
Robert Fuller Lane	8943 Old Chelmsford
Julius Styles Road	343 Trinity Durham
Anne Cromwell Inverness	85 High Lane

As you can see, flat files contain raw data.

However, the file is structured by limiting each field to a certain number of characters.

The assigned characteristics are set in stone by the creator.

This means that whatever program you use to read and process flat files needs to be able to detect each field separately and identify the information. Keep in mind that, in this case, we are not dealing with a database per se.

We don't have the typical structure which defines the separation between the fields. This means that the information is read directly, and therefore, flat files can be processed extremely fast.

However, there is a downside. To manipulate the information from a flat-file, you need to use specialized tools that detect where certain data is stored.

This means that you should opt for flat files only when creating smaller lists of data items. The more complex your system is, the more difficult it becomes to read the file and manipulate its data.

Databases may take somewhat longer to process, but unlike flat-file systems, they are more versatile because you can increase their size as needed.

Additionally, the programs that work with databases are far more versatile and will work no matter the operating system you're using.

While flat files have their use, databases are easier to handle when developing a program. A software developer won't need to know all the details about how the file stores the data.

That is what a database management system is for. It will deal with all the data manipulation, while the tools you use on flat files need to include the same functions in their code.

In other words, when working with flat files, you will need to include their data manipulation code in all the different tools you're using.

This is not the case when it comes to databases because the database management system does all of this for you.

Any other tools you need to use can work with the data without including the same data manipulation code.

Furthermore, some programs that include the data manipulation features for flat files will only run on a particular system, which means that the user would have to migrate the program to a different system that is currently in use.

This is time-consuming. There are differences in code when it comes to different operating systems.

Database Types

The very first database models were built using a hierarchy-based structure.

This lead to several problems, including the fact that such databases were not easy to modify and maintain due to their inflexibility.

The structural issue and various redundancy problems have led to the development of a network type database.

Its purpose was to eliminate such imperfections.

They indeed offered the advantage of a near lack in redundancy; however, to achieve this quality another sacrifice had to be made.

The structure of a network model database was highly complex and therefore led to another set of problems.

An answer to these technical issues was soon offered with the development of the relational database.

The structure was simple, and minimal redundancy was one of its main features.

With the creation of this new database type, SQL entered the stage.

Its purpose was to turn the relational databases into something revolutionary and send the other models into obscurity.

The Relational Database

The first relational model was developed in the 70s by Edgar Frank Codd from IBM; however, it started seeing the light of day commercially only 10 years later.

With a new type of database, a new database management system was needed. This is how Oracle came to be: a new answer given by a small startup company.

At this point, relational databases entered the mainstream. This made possible the ability to modify the structure of this model without changing the design of the programs used on the other database types.

For instance, to create more columns inside the database table, all you needed to do was add them to it without any other time-consuming modifications. The applications that relied on the database did not require any changes.

Another powerful advantage was the fact that some data could be stored in one table while other data could be in a different table.

Neither of these tables had to be connected in any way. Therefore, you could change the information in one of them without affecting negatively the other.

Now that you know the background of the relational model, let's explore the components of a relational database and see what it's made of.

First, imagine your friends and family gathering at your table. These are your personal relations, and databases have them as well; however, each element has a table of its own.

In other words, a relational database is constructed using some relations (at least one). You can analyze these database relations as an array that contains only columns and rows. This 2-dimensional array would contain unique rows filled with one value per cell.

If you have issues understanding this aspect, think of an Excel spreadsheet containing the statistics of your favorite athletes. You will have a number of columns that represent a player's stats, such as the number of seasons played, the number of games, scores, misses, and so on.

These columns are unique for all rows and will never change their meaning. The rows contain the values for each one of these statistics. This spreadsheet data can also be inserted into a relational database.

Take note that the order in which you introduce the data items doesn't matter. There's no need to follow an alphabetical order or anything similar.

When you use a database management system to handle the information, it will process everything at once without searching for some kind of hierarchy.

Another aspect that all databases share is something often referred to as a "view." It might not involve a beautiful landscape, however, it does provide you with the visual satisfaction of seeing the many columns and rows of data you create. Keep in mind that database tables don't necessarily involve all of the data they contain.

You can limit them to only the columns and rows you are interested in or the ones that fit certain requirements for a project. To put aside the information you don't want, you need to build a view.

In essence, this is a version of your database that can be processed and manipulated by several programs. Also known as virtual tables, the views can be constructed using either certain data from one table or from several tables that aren't connected. This means that views are no different than any table. Programs and users see them the same way.

However, there is one characteristic that sets them apart. The tables are part of the information itself; they are independent structures. The views, on the other hand, provide you with the ability to examine the data visually, but they are not part of it.

Let's take a look at an example to gain a better understanding of views. We have one database that contains 2 different tables, one called "client" and another one called "invoice." The first table contains several columns that hold data about the client, such as client ID, name, address, phone number, and so on.

The second table contains information such as the invoice number, client ID, sale, type of payment, and so on. Now let's say your supervisor comes in to find out a client's name, address, and number.

Nothing else is of interest to him. In this case, you don't show him the tables. That would be a waste of his valuable time searching through a great deal of information to find something so specific.

This is what views are for. You use the "client" table to create a view that holds only the data he's interested in, namely the columns he asked for. All you need to do is specify the view to limit the rows and columns it pulls out of the database.

As you can see in this example, views are extremely useful because you can separate the data you need from possibly millions of data items you don't need. You can also format this information safely, knowing that the data itself is not modified.

As mentioned earlier, the operations you perform on the data inside a view does not affect the database itself. Furthermore, using a view instead of the database tables can also serve as a security measure because there might be some information you are not allowed to show.

With that in mind, let's explore the components that form such a database because there's more involved than just tables. Database information is maintained through a well-defined structure composed of a schema, domain, and constraints.

The schema handles the way the database's tables are arranged, the domain tells us which values can be stored inside of a column, and the constraints are used to limit various users from introducing the wrong information inside the table.

Let's analyze this structure in more detail:

- **Schema:** This is essentially the structure itself, also known as the conceptual view or logical view.

    It is also the component of the database that represents the metadata. As you already know, metadata is what provides us with information about the database. It describes the structure, the tables, and everything that is stored within them. Therefore, you can say that metadata is, in fact, data on its own.

- **Domain:** Each table column has an attribute that involves several values. The collection of these values represents the domain of that attribute.

    For instance, let's say you have a database that contains many different car models. The tables for these cars will include a column called "color." Now let's say there's a Nissan Qashqai that comes in several different colors such as metallic silver, black, pearl white, and cherry red.

    All of these colors together represent the color attribute's domain.

- **Constraints:** They are as important as all the other components, however, they are often underappreciated and ignored, especially by those who just start in the technical world of databases.

  As the name suggests, a database's constraints define which values can belong to an attribute. The primary function of a constraint is to limit various users from introducing the wrong information in the table.

  Keep in mind that all of these values that do belong to a certain domain must also comply with the constraints we set for each column. Applying constraints to a column is like applying rigid restrictions.

  This means that the domain of a column is determined not only by the values themselves but by the constraints as well. In our example, with the car model database, we can introduce a constraint to force the column with the color values to accept no more than 4 values.

  Therefore, if another user tries to add more colors to the list, they will not be accepted. Such data entry limitations are practical in such cases because you don't want someone to introduce certain values that don't exist.

Imagine an employee adding mint green to one of the models when the manufacturer doesn't offer that color.

This information can be passed further to potential customers who will eventually, as a result, end up disappointed when they find out that their chosen color only exists due to a faulty database entry.

Relational databases have been the height of data storage for a long time, and their success has kept them in use to this day. While they may no longer be the mainstream choice for most users and companies, you might still stumble upon them once in a while.

However, they do not offer a solution to every problem. There are various limits to this model. In the past couple of decades, object-oriented programming through languages like C, Java, and C++ has made it obvious that more can be achieved.

These programming languages are far more powerful than the ones at the time when relational databases became the norm. They can solve complex problems, and they offer advanced features such as inheritance, encapsulations, object identity, and much more.

We are not going to expand on object-oriented programming because that is not the purpose of this book; however, you should understand that many of these modern features cannot be used with the relational model.

This means new database management systems had to be created to take advantage of the new techniques. The object model was created as a response to the new possibilities; however, it never became popular.

Keep in mind that object-oriented programming is the most popular type of programming in today's tech industries across the board; however, the object model brought new issues that kept it from growing on its own.

This new database type was soon after combined with the relational model to create the object-relational model.

The Object-Relational Database

Both the relation model and the object model offered an array of advantages.

Fortunately, the developers at the time thought about the possibility of profiting from the power of object-oriented databases, as well as the compatibility offered by the relational model. This is how the object-relational database came to be.

In essence, it takes the relational model, and it adds to it the functionality of the object model.

The object-oriented characteristics have been implemented using SQL and therefore allow all database management systems to adapt to becoming object-relational database management systems.

Keep in mind that they still retain compatibility with the original relational model.

Since the 90s, the relational database has been gradually expanded by introducing more and more object-oriented features as the programming techniques and languages continued to develop.

However, at the heart of this type of database, the relational model remained true while it received several extensions over the years.

Relational databases started dropping in popularity in favor of the standard SQL databases we use today.

Modern problems required complex SQL solutions that could only be provided by the object-oriented features.

Chapter 2: Basic Background of SQL

When you look at the structure of any business, you will see that it generates, holds, and then uses data.

Because of the different ways that the company will need to handle this data, they will need to find some method of storing the information.

In the traditional methods, known as Database Management System or DBMS, business organizations would have all the data in one place to help them out.

These systems are pretty simple to use, but modern technology has forced some changes.

Even the most essential or basic data management systems have changed, and now they are more powerful than before.

This can be an advantage to some companies that have a large amount of data to keep track of or who may need to be careful with some sensitive information.

Out of all this, there was a new breed of data management that has been implemented known as the Relational Database Management System or RDBMS.

This was derived from the renowned traditional DBMS, but it is going to have some more to do with the web as well as server and client technologies.

This means that they are going to help various companies with the management of data.

One of these new relational databases that will help to store the data in an easy and simple to use a method that also keeps it all safe is SQL.

What Is SQL?

The first question that you may have is what is SQL. It is best to start at the beginning. SQL stands for "Structured Query Language," and it is a simple language to learn, considering it will allow interaction to occur between various databases found in a particular system.

The original version was established in the 1970s. This continued to progress in 1,979 until IBM released a new prototype, the Relational Software Inc. that published one of the first SQL tools in the world.

This tool was at first called ORACLE, and it gained so much success that the company was able to split off from IBM and create the Oracle Corporation. Even today, ORACLE is one of the leaders thanks to being able to use the SQL language.

The SQL is a set of instructions that you can use to interact with your relational database. While there are a lot of languages that you can use to do this, SQL is the only language that most databases can understand.

Whenever you are ready to interact with one of these databases, the software can go in and translate the commands that you are given, whether you are giving them in form entries or mouse clicks.

These will be translated into SQL statements that the database will already be able to interpret. If you have ever worked with a database-driven software program, then it is likely that you have used some form of SQL in the past.

Likely, you didn't even know that you were doing this, though. For example, there are a lot of dynamic web pages that are database driven.

These will take some user input from the forms and clicks that you are making and then will use this information to compose a SQL query.

This query will then go through and retrieve the information from the database to act, such as switch over to a new page.

To illustrate how this functions, think about a simple online catalog that allows you to search. The search page will often contain a form that will just have a text box.

You can enter the name of the item that you would like to search using the form, and then you would simply need to click on the search button. As soon as you click on the search button, the web server will go through and search through the database to find anything related to that search term.

It will bring those back to create a new web page that will go along with your specific request. For those who have not spent that much time at all learning a programming language and who would not consider themselves programmers, the commands that you would use in SQL are not too hard to learn.

Commands in SQL are all designed with a syntax that fits in with the English language. At first, this will seem complicated, and you may be worried about how much work it will be to get it set up. But when you start to work on a few codes, you will find that it is not that hard to work with.

Often, just reading out the SQL statement will help you to figure out what the command will do.

How This Works With Your Database

If you decide that SQL is the language that you will work on for managing your database, you can take a look at the database. The database has lots of information.

There are a ton of things that SQL can help you with when it comes to managing your database, and you will see some great results.

Take the example of a phone book. It is a database that has lots of information like names, the company they work for, address, and phone number.

Such information is contained in one single area for ease of access and avoids time wastage. This is similar to an SQL database.

Why Is SQL So Great?

Within the various types of database management systems that you can work with, it is time to discuss why you would want to choose SQL over some of the other options that are out there.

You not only have the option of working with other databases but also with other coding languages, and there are benefits to choosing each one. So, why would you want to work with SQL in particular?

Some of the great benefits that you can get from using SQL as your database management system includes:

Incredibly Fast

If you would like to pick out a management system that can sort through the information quickly and will get the results back in no time, then SQL is one of the best programs to use for this.

You will be surprised at how much information you can get back, and how quickly it will come back to you.

In fact, out of all the options, this is the most efficient one that you can go with.

Well-Defined Standards

The database that comes with SQL is one that has been working well for a long time.

Also, it has been able to develop some good standards that ensure the database is strong and works the way that you want.

Some of the other databases that you may want to work with will miss out on these standards, and this can be frustrating when you use them.

You Do Not Need a Lot of Coding

If you are looking into the SQL database, you do not need to be an expert in coding to get the work done.

We will take a look at a few codes that can help, but even a beginner will get these down and do well when working in SQL.

Keeps Your Stuff Organized

When it comes to running your business, it is important that you can keep your information safe and secure as well as organized.

And while there are a ton of great databases that you can go with, none will work as well as the SQL language at getting this all done.

Object-Oriented DBMS

The database of SQL relies on the DBMS system that we talked about earlier because this will make it easier to find the information that you are searching for, to store the right items, and to do so much more within the database.

You Can Earn a Lot of Money

You always want to earn more when you work for an organization. You can certainly get a better salary if you know how to use SQL. You can do this by either nurturing your programming skills in SQL or by learning how to maintain a system and keep it running effectively and efficiently.

You can also work as an SQL analyst and provide information and insights for a business; it will help the seniors make better decisions. This will help to maximize the profits for any business.

All Types of Technology Uses SQL

Most businesses use database tools and technologies like MySQL, Microsoft SQL Server, and PostgreSQL. You should also remember that most people use SQL at some point in their lives.

If you are not aware, you also use SQL on your smartphone.

Employers Look for SQL Skills

Most employers actively look for people who know how to use SQL. Yes, an employer is willing to pay you more, but he or she also is aware of the benefits of hiring an individual who is skilled at using SQL.

If you want to move jobs or change your area of work, you should learn how to code in SQL. You will be one of the most sought-after candidates for the position

The benefits that you can get when you choose to work with the SQL program. While some people do struggle with this interface in the beginning, but overall there are a ton of good features to work on with SQL, and you will really enjoy how fast and easy it is to work with this language and its database.

Working on the Databases

Within this language, databases are going to be groups of information.

Some will consider these databases as organized mechanisms that can store information so that the user can access the data effectively and efficiently to avoid issues.

There are many times that you are using databases without even realizing it.

For example, a phone book can be a database because it contains a lot of information about people, such as physical addresses, phone numbers, and names all in one place and it is in alphabetical order to make it easier for everyone to find the information, or the pieces of data, that you need easily.

A Relational Database

A relational database is going to be segregated into logical units or tables.

The tables can then be interconnected inside of your database to make the most sense for what you are working on.

These databases make it so that you can break up your data into smaller units.

This makes it easier to maintain the database and make it more optimized for all the different uses for your organization.

The relational database is important because it will help to keep everything together, but splits it up enough that the pieces are a bit smaller.

The server is going to be able to go through all of the parts to find what you need because it is easier to go through smaller pieces rather than the bigger ones.

This is why so many systems have chosen to go over to a relational database for their customers.

Client and Server Technology

In the past, if you were working with a computer for your business, you were most likely using a mainframe computer.

What this means is that the machines were able to hold onto a large system, and this system would be good at storing all the information that you need and for processing options.

The user would be able to get onto these computers and interact with the mainframe, which in this case would be a "dumb" terminal or one that is not able to interact all on its own.

The dumb terminal would need to rely on all the information that is inside the computer, such as the memory, processor, and storage, to get the information to show up the correct function.

Now, these systems were able to work, and they got the job done for a very long time.

If your company uses these, and this is what you are most comfortable with using, it does get the work done. But some options on the market will do a better job. These options can be found in the client-server system.

These systems will use some different processes to help you to get the results that are needed. With this one, the main computer that you are using, which would be called the "server," will be accessible to any user who is on the network.

Now, these users must have the right credentials to do this, which helps to keep the system safe and secure.

But if the user has the right information and is on your network, they can reach the information without a lot of trouble and barely any effort.

The user can get the server from other servers or their desktop computer, and the user will then be known as the "client" so that the client and server are easily able to interact through this database.

The big difference that you will find between the client/server environments and the mainframe is that the former is going to allow the computer of the user to think on its own. The computer will be able to run its applications rather than having to rely on the server all the time.

Because of these great features, many businesses are moving over to the client/server environment to make things easier.

Internet-Based Database Systems

For the most part, the different database systems are moving towards the idea of using integration with the internet.

The users will be able to access this database going through the internet, which means that the users can check out the database of the company simply being on their web browsers.

Customers, or anyone who is using the data, will be able to perform changes on the account, check the status of any transactions, check inventories, pay online, and purchase items.

All of this can be done from their web browsers, which makes the transaction smoother.

To see these databases, you will just need to go on a web browser of your choice, go into the company's website, if required you will need to log in to your account, and then search for any of the information that you need.

Many of the businesses that you will work with require their customers to create this account with them before being able to go through the different steps, mostly for security reasons to protect their payment information and more.

You will often get the usernames and passwords for free as a customer, but it can help to protect your information.

Of course, there are a lot of things that happen in this system that are behind the scenes when the customer gets into an internet-based database.

While the customer is going to be able to access some basic information such as their payment information and what they have ordered, there are a lot of things that the server was going to have to put together to make this information come up on the screen.

For example, you may find that the web browser will go through and execute SQL to find the data that the user is requesting.

The SQL will be utilized to reach the database that the customer has put in place, such as a list of clothing or food that they are trying to sell, and then the SQL will be able to give this information back to the website server before relaying that data to the web browser of the user.

This all takes some time to get to work together, even though it often takes just a few seconds to have it show up on the screen.

All of the things that were listed above will have to occur simply for a search result to come back or for you to be able to look through your payment information.

You may see a simple expression come up on the screen after you do a quick search, but there is so much that is going to go on in the background.

SQL is going to help you to make all of this possible. It is the way that you can store your information and ensure that you will get the right information to the user when they need it the most.

Chapter 3: Installation

Let us start by defining what SQL servers mean. SQL server refers to an RDMS (Relational Database Management System) that was invented by Microsoft a few years ago.

Seemingly, the primary reason SQL server was developed and designed was to give competition to the Oracle database as well as MySQL.

This server has been modified and well advanced to support ANSI SQL, a type of Structured Query Language.

SQL servers, however, are equipped with their tactics of implementing the T-SQL programming language. You might be wondering what T-SQL means.

Well, it is a proprietary programming language developed by Microsoft, which is commonly known as the Transactional SQL.

This server has been equipped with the ability to declare variable, exquisite handling as well as stored procedures. It is the primary interface tool of SQL servers in the SSMS (Server Management Studio). It has been modified in a way that can support the 32-bit environment as well as that containing a 64-bit environment.

This chapter seeks to discuss more SQL servers, and at the end of it, you will have a better understanding of how it works.

Read on to find out!

Installing Oracle Database

This tutorial will guide you on the procedure of installing an oracle server. It has been simplified for quick and easy comprehension.

To have the Oracle database installed on your computer, you first have to download the app from the Oracle website's download page.

This should be a quick process because the Oracle database does not contain a lot of files and, therefore, smaller in size.

Once you have installed the data, which should preferably be in a ZIP format, the next thing you ought to do is to extract those files in a specific folder on your computer.

You should also ensure your computer is free from viruses and other potential threats that could harm the Oracle database.

If the installation process is successful, your computer will alert you through a pop-up screen message.

You need to note that to start the installation process, you have to click on the setup.exe file that you saved in the data we mentioned earlier.

This process has been broken down into the following steps, each carrying significant procedures needed for it to run efficiently.

Read on!

Step 1: During the process of installing the Oracle database, the installer will ask you to fill in the email address you often use as a means of keeping things secure.

If you do not want to provide your email address, you can opt to skip this process by clicking the "next button."

When you chose not to fill in your email address, the Oracle installer will not prompt you with the above pop up message, but it will install provide a "continue" option that will you to the next step.

Step 2: In this step, the installer will inquire whether you prefer creating and configuring a database, installing a software database only, or upgrading the already operating database.

Now that we have never installed the Oracle database before select option one and then press the next button.

Step 3: In this step, the Oracle installer will let you choose a preferable system database.

Considering that we only installed Oracle on the computer but not the actual server, you will, therefore, opt for option one: the desktop-class and then click the "Next" button.

Step 4: This fourth step will let you identify the account on your Windows that you will install and attach the Oracle database for a more secure system.

In this option, it is recommended you go for option 3, which is using the Windows built on the account.

Step 5: This is the step that lets you indicate the specific folder the Oracle database you downloaded will be installed.

Secondly, it will give you a chance to create a global database name as well as a password.

Lastly, it also provides a platform for you to come up with a pluggable username file.

Step 6: This step of the Oracle installation process is where the installer runs quick and prerequisite checkups on the software.

Step 7: In this step, the Oracle installer will give a summary of the complete information, including the database system and global settings.

It is recommended that you review that information before going ahead and installing it; doing so ensures that you don't make any mistakes.

Step 8: This is the step where the Oracle installer initiates the procedure of installing the database.

This takes a short time to complete. It, however, depends on the speed of your computer.

Once this process is done, you will be able to view the DCA (Database Configuration Assistant).

The next step involves you clicking on the password management button that will enable you to provide a password for the Oracle accounts.

Lastly, this step will see your key in the password you created for the System & SYS accounts, and finally, hit the OK button.

Step 9: Now that the installation process has been completed successfully, you will be informed by the installer, of course, that the process is done and you can close the tab. Do so by clicking on "close."

Installing the SQL Developer

This section of the chapter will give you a clear outline of how you can download and install an SQL developer on your computer.

For your information, the installation of SQL developer doesn't need an installer.

Instead, it requires you to unzip a particular tool. There are various types of appliances, including the info-zip device and the platform unzip tool. They are all available on the official zip website.

You are, however, warned not to install any SQL database into an already existing Oracle device.

This is because the Oracle Home database cannot be uninstalled using that actively operating universal installer.

Additionally, if you are using an updated version of the SQL developer, and you want to continue using that version after installing the recognized app, you need to first unzip the release kit to various databases that were previously used for the older version.

In case the Oracle database has been installed as well, a newer version of that particular app is installed, as well.

Additionally, a specific version of the developer is involved and can be accessed through the side menu located under the Oracle.

You, however, need to note that this kind of SQL developer is not the same as any other SQL file that you download and unzip from the Oracle website.

For this to work more efficiently, you are advised to first create and customize a folder on your computer, make sure it is free from viruses and place your downloaded files there.

When downloading the SQL database files on a Windows computer, you will come across 2 different kits: the first one on which the systems run containing the Sun Java SDK and the other one that doesn't include the Sun Java SDK.

Make sure you are downloading the right file first before installing it. You are welcome to confirm from the upcoming part of this section vital instructions and requirements needed to install the SQL server.

To begin with, the procedure of installing a SQL database mainly depends on one thing: whether or not the Windows system in use doesn't contain the Sun Java SDK.

When working on a Windows system with the release 1.5.0_06 or installed later, follow the necessary steps. Every other system, including the Mac OS and Linux that have no Java SDK, have their specific procedure.

Below we discuss ways you can install the SQL servers on any computer, be it Windows or Linux.

Read on to find out!

When you want to be run and install your SQL developer on Windows operating systems, and the Java script involved is more than the standard update 6, you are recommended to implement the following steps.

Start by unzipping the SQL developer file to the folder you have preferred.

For instance, it can be C:\Program Files. On other computers, it can also be referred to as the SQL developer installer.

Once you have unzipped the kit containing the SQL developer, it will trigger a folder named the "sqldevlp" to be established the installed SQL file formed earlier.

It will also result in various folders and files being located in the same directory.

If you wish to start running this SQL developer, it is recommended you go to the previously installed SQL folder and then click the "sqldevlper.exe" file.

Upon clicking, you will be asked to key in the name for your Java file downloaded earlier, then proceed to click the known corresponding file named program files java folds.

When the SQL developer database starts operating, you can as well link to a database of your choice by only right-clicking the connections option in the known connections navigator, then following it up by choosing a new connection model. Similarly, if you had a few exported connections in the database, it is recommended you import those connections and put them into use.

In case you wish to know more about SQL development, you can click on the SQL developer and then the Help option, next click on the table of contents.

This will prompt a drop-down containing various topics that informs you about the SQL developer.

Choose a topic you want to know more about under the category SQL developer concepts

Moving on, we next discuss how you can install the SQL developer on Linux and Mac OS systems.

To start, you need to know that the SQL developer only needs the Sun Java J2SE to be installed on the operating system.

Therefore, if you want to install the file on those devices, proceed to the Java website and download its data.

Next, click on the downloaded link to update JDK 5.0 or, rather, the most recently updated file. To install the file on your computer, you recommended following the following steps.

Start by unzipping the kit containing SQL developer into a folder of your choice. This directory will be directed to a folder named the "sqldeveloper_installer."

Just like the previous installing procedure, unzipping this file will prompt a new folder to be created under the data and might also cause several files to be placed in the same directory.

If you wish to start running the SQL developer on these devices, you are advised to go through the "sqldeveloper installer" directory and perform one of the following procedures to your operating systems: on both Windows and Linux, start by double-clicking the mode of connection and choosing a new connection.

Additionally, if you have had a previously installed SQL table, you can click on the Help table to learn more about the existing features of your database.

Using the SQL Developer

This section of the chapter seeks to discuss the ways and methods you can be able to use the Oracle SQL developer.

You can use it to modify a database design, go through objects and create them, and importing or exporting the database linkages.

Let us start by defining an Oracle SQL developer: It refers to a free tool that deals with graphics, making it easier to operate with the Oracle databases, and it is the most recommended tool for Oracle databases.

As we will find out later in this section, it is easier for the user to modify or review the database design using this platform.

When using the SQL developer, you can link it to any version of the Oracle database or, preferably, a more upgraded one.

If you wish to connect it to am an older version of the database, you have to choose a different tool like SQL Plus which was described in the various sections.

How to Create a Database Connection

You have to create a new connection set first before working with any database.

Upon starting the SQL developer, the linkage screen will display every database connection available. You might be wondering how you can be able to create a new connection, and we discuss that next!

To come up with a new, unique database, you are recommended to apply a procedure described in section 3.2.

Upon installation of software that this book has described in the previous sections, the operating system will promptly be available on your system.

At the end of it, you will be in a position to build connections for the users installed earlier.

To be more specific, it is recommended that you use the AP devices to modify the tables and databases.

Once you have created the database connection, you should make sure the passwords and usernames are unique and robust enough to keep off hackers.

It also has a provision where it does not matter whether you are keying in the letters in lower or uppercase.

It will prevent you from having issues, especially when you forget your password.

How to Import or Export Database Connection

If you aim to copy several database links from several computers, it can be done so by exporting the database linkages through an XML file, as described in the previous sections. You can then apply the XML file in importing database linkages to a different computer.

For instance, you can export data linkages from AP and EX users to different users in the system. Consequently, if you wish, the same technique can still be applied and displayed. It takes a few steps to ensure the stored connections and links are kept in a particular file.

There are a few dialog boxes that can be used to create database connections. Follow the steps below to create a new database:

Step 1: Click twice on the node of connections located in the window connection then click the new connections command to show the essential dialogue box needed in coming up with the database connections.

Step 2: Start by entering a connection username as well as a password for the recommended connection.

Step 3: In this step, you can click on the test button to test whether the connection is working or not.

If you followed the right procedure, and the connection ends up working, you will be informed of the success through a pop-up message located just above the Help button.

Step 4: This is the last step of the connection process. It is a step where you are required to save the settings. To do so, you can click on the Save button.

Once you do that, a new connection will be introduced in the connections window area.

Creating a MySQL Database

This is typically a simple and interesting thing to do once you master the basics of MySQL.

Choose between the phpMyAdmin interface or Secure Shell Command-Line.

Database Structure

There are different items for different components of the system.

We call these components objects, and our challenge as a data professional is to use the appropriate objects, or ingredients if you are hungry, to satisfy the needs of our client—an end-user or an application.

This book focuses on 2 types of objects—tables and views.

Tables

An SQL table is defined as a container present in a given database where one can store their data.

Some will be very simple, and others will have many components to them. You decide how you want to describe your data; each item you want to describe is a table.

Let's talk about some of the basic structures of a table. I think it will be helpful to continue the comparison to the sandwich counter. We mentioned that each container was a specific size and had a specific purpose.

I shouldn't put meat in the lettuce container, and the reverse is also true. In the case of a table, I have these containers, and I need to put something specific in each one.

Each container is represented by a column, and the specific type of data that goes inside the column is called a data type.

Columns and Data Types

The blessing and curse of the relational database system are you can describe in simple terms or very complex terms the data in a table.

There is a joke among database administrators that for all the features in relational database systems, the most popular database software in the world is Microsoft Excel.

Part of this is because it is so easy to start categorizing and describing our data; however, in a real sense, this is how data is broken up in our relational database system. Each piece of information we want to track is put into a column and those columns have specific data requirements.

Our data requirements are called Data Types. They help describe the type of information we are looking to put in our column—text, a date, a number, a yes/no field.

Once we establish a data type, other types of data will not be allowed in that column.

Views

Views are queries we save for later use. They normally remove the complexity of the database from an end-user, so it makes it easier to get to the data.

We can pull information from a view using a select statement; however, views don't contain data and are based on tables.

Some RDMBS systems have indexed views that do contain data; however, that is beyond the scope of this book.

Rows

The item we are trying to collect data on, and all the information about the item, make up our row. This is also sometimes called a record.

Primary Keys

Used to make a given row unique for ease of identification.

Most often this is a number that simply increments as a new row is added, but has no meaning to the data in the table. Sometimes a primary key can be used from the data we are collecting—we can identify a column that will not repeat.

Primary Keys become very important when we try to relate one table to another.

Schema

A schema is the owner of a database object.

As we are just beginning, all the objects in the database will have only one owner; however, if you use third-party applications, you might see additional schema owners. Schemas are helpful when we want to apply security to a database.

Microsoft Access does not have a concept of Schemas.

Chapter 4: Data Types

Certain types of data can be found in the 4 main databases that SQL is used in.

Listed below are the data types that can be found in each kind of database.

It is important and can be very useful to have an accurate list of the very different kinds of data types.

Access Data Types

Listed below are the different types of data that can be found and used in SQL and what properties they possess and how much storage is contained.

- **Byte:** Allows numbers from the range of 0–255 to be contained. Storage is 1 byte.
- **Currency:** This holds 15 whole dollar digits with additional decimal places up to 4. The storage is 8 bytes.
- **Date/Time:** Will be used for dates and times. The storage is 8 bytes.

- **Double:** This is a double-precision floating-point that will handle most decimals. The storage is 8 bytes.
- **Integer:** This will allow the amounts between -32,768 and 32,767. Storage is 2 bytes.
- **Text:** This is used for combinations of texts and numbers. This can up to 255 characters to be stored.
- **Memo:** This can be used for the text of larger amounts. It can store 65,536 characters. Memo fields can't be sorted, but they can be searched.
- **Long:** This will allow between -2,147,483, 648 and 2,147,483,647 whole numbers. Storage is 4 bytes.
- **Single:** This is a single-precision floating-point that will handle most decimals. Storage is 4 bytes.
- **AutoNumber:** This field can automatically give each record of data its number, which usually starts at 1. Storage is 4 bytes.
- **Yes/No:** This is a logical field that can be displayed as yes/no, true/false, or on/off. The use of true and false should be equivalent to -1, and 0. In these fields, null values are not allowed. Storage is 1 bit.
- **Ole Object:** This can store BLOBS such as pictures, audio, video. BLOBs are Binary Large Objects. The storage is 1 gigabyte (GB).

- **Hyperlink:** This contains links to other files like web pages.
- **Lookup Wizard:** This will let you make an options list. A drop-down list will then allow it to be chosen. Storage is 4 bytes.

MySQL Data Types

Data types can differ between different types of databases.

Data is grouped into 3 categories:

- Character
- Number
- Date/Time

Character Data Types

- **CHAR(size):** A fixed-length string can be held with this data type. It can hold special characters, letters, and numbers. This can store up to 255 characters.
- **VARCHAR(size):** This can hold a variable string length that can hold special characters, letters, and numbers. The size will be specified in the parenthesis. It can store up to 255 characters. This will automatically be a text

type that is converted to if the value is placed higher than 255 characters.
- **TINYTEXT:** This holds a string with 255 characters of maximum length.
- **TEXT:** This holds a string with 65,535 characters of maximum length.
- **MEDIUMTEXT:** This holds a string with 16,777,215 maximum characters.
- **LONGTEXT:** This holds a string with 4,294,967,295 maximum characters.
- **BLOB:** These hold 65,535 bytes of maximum data.
- **MEDIUMBLOB:** These hold 16,777,215 bytes of maximum data.
- **LONGBLOB:** These hold 4,294,967,295 bytes of maximum data.
- **ENUM(x,y,z, etc.):** A list that contains possible values. This list can hold 65535 max values. When a value is entered into the list that isn't contained inside that list, a blank value will be entered instead. The order that the values are entered is how they will also be sorted.
- **SET:** This is similar to the ENUM data type. This data type holds a maximum of 64 list items and can store more than one choice.

Number Data Types

The most common of the options are listed below, along with their storage type when it comes to bytes and values:

- **TINYINT(size):** Holds -128 to 127, or 0 to 255 unsigned.
- **SMALLINT(size):** Holds -32768 to 32767, or 0 to 65535 unsigned.
- **MEDIUMINT(size):** Holds -8388608 to 8388607, or 16,777,215 unsigned.
- **INT(size):** Holds -2,147,483,648 to 2,147,483,647, or 4,294,967,295 unsigned.
- **BIGINT(size):** Holds -9,223,372,036,854,775,808 to 9,223,372,036,854,775,807 or 18,446,744,073,709,551,615 unsigned.
- **FLOAT(size,d):** This is a tiny number with a decimal point that can float. Specified in the size parameter is the maximum amount of digits. Specified in the d parameter is the maximum amount of digits in the right of the decimal point.
- **DOUBLE(size,d):** This is a large number with a decimal point that floats. The maximum number of digits may be specified in the size parameter (size). The

maximum number of digits to the right of the decimal point is specified in the d parameter (d).

- **DECIMAL(size,d):** This type is a string that is stored, which allows a decimal point that is fixed. The maximum number of digits may be specified in the size parameter (size). Specified in the d parameter is the maximum amount of digits to the right of the decimal point.

An extra option is found in integer types that are called unsigned.

Normally, an integer will go from a value of negative to positive.

When adding the unsigned attribute will be able to move the range up higher so that it will not start at a negative number, but a zero.

That is why the unsigned option is mentioned after the specified numbers listed for the different data types.

Date/Time Data Types

The options for dates are:

- **DATE():** This is to enter a date in the format of YYYY-MM-DD as in 2016-04-19 (April 19th, 2016)

- **DATETIME():** This is to enter a combination of date and time in the format of YYYY-MM-DD and HH:MM:SS as in 13:30:26 (1:30 p.m. at 26 seconds)
- **TIMESTAMP():** This is to enter to store the number of seconds and match the current time zone. The format is YYYY-MM-DD HH:MM:SS.
- **TIME():** This will allow you to enter the time. The format is HH:MM:SS.
- **YEAR():** This is to enter a year in a 2 or four-digit format. A four-digit format would be as 2016 or 1992. A two-digit format would be as 72 or 13.

It is important to note that if the DATETIME and TIMESTAMP will return to the same format.

When compared to each other, they will still work in different ways.

The TIMESTAMP will automatically update to the current time and date of the time zone present TIMESTAMP will also accept other various formats available such as YYYYMMDDHHMMSS, YYMMDDHHMMSS, YYYYMMDD, and also YYMMDD.

Oracle Data Types

Character Data Types

- **Char(size):** This stores strings of fixed lengths. The number of characters to store will be in the size parameter, with a maximum of 2,000 bytes in size.
- **Nchar(size):** This stores NLS strings of fixed lengths. The size is the number of characters to store with the maximum size of 2,000 bytes.
- **Nvarchar2(size):** This stores NLS strings of a variable-length. The number of characters to store will be in the size parameter with a maximum of 4,000 bytes in size.
- **Varchar2(size):** This stores strings of variable lengths. The number of characters to store will be in the size parameter with the maximum size of 2 GB.
- **Long:** This stores strings of variable lengths. The size is the number of characters to store with a maximum size of 2 GB.
- **Raw:** This stores binary strings of variable lengths with a maximum size of 2,000 bytes.
- **Long raw:** This stores binary strings of variable lengths with a maximum size of 2 GB.

Number Data Types

- **Integer:** This is an ANSI datatype that is equivalent to NUMBER(38).
- **Int:** This is an ANSI datatype equivalent to NUMBER(38).
- **Smallint:** This is an ANSI datatype equivalent to NUMBER(38).
- **Number(p,s):** This is to store a number. From 1–38 is what it can range from 84–127 is what the scale can range from.
- **Numeric(p,s):** This is to store a number. From 1–38 is what it can range from.
- **Float:** This is an ANSI datatype that is a number with a floating-point and with binary precision. The default for this data type is 126 binary or 38 decimal.
- **Dec(p,s):** This is to store a number that can range from 1–38.
- **Decimal(p,s):** This is to store a number that can range from 1–38.
- **Real:** This is an ANSI datatype to store a number with a floating-point and with binary precision. The default for this data type is 63 binary or 18 decimal. This is also equivalent to FLOAT(63).

- **Double precision:** This is an ANSI datatype that is a binary number with a floating-point. The default for this data type is 126 binary and is also equivalent to FLOAT(126).

Large Object (LOB) Data Types

- **Bfile:** These are file locators that will point to the file that is binary on the system of the server file, which is outside of the database. The maximum file size is 264-1 bytes.
- **Blob:** This stores large objects that are binary and unstructured. These can store up to 4 GB -1.
- **Clob:** This stores character data of single-byte and multiple-byte. They can store up to 4 GB -1.
- **Nclob:** This stores Unicode data. It can store up to 4 GB -1.

Date/Time Data Types

- **Date:** This is used to store a date anywhere between January 1st, 4712 BC, and December 31st, 9999 AD.
- **Timestamp:** This is for storing fractional second's precision. It must be between 0 and 9, and 6 is the default. This includes seconds, minute, hour, day, month, and year.

- **Timestamp with time zone:** This is for storing fractional second's precision. It must be between 0 and 9, and 6 is the default. This includes the year, month, day, hour, minute, and seconds as well as the time zone.
- **Timestamp with local time zone:** This is for storing fractional second's precision. It must be a number between 0 and 9, and the default is 6. This includes the year, month, day, hour, minute, seconds, along expressed time zone.
- **Interval year to month:** This is for storing year precision, and the year will be the number of digits with 2 as the default. This is for the years and months stored in the time.
- **Interval day to seconds:** This is for storing day precision and must be between 0 and 9, with 6 as the default. This also includes the precision of fractional seconds and must also be between 0 and 9, with the default being 6. This is for a period that will be stored in the format of days, hours, minutes, and seconds.

SQL Server

Character Data Types

- **Char(n):** This is for storing a fixed-length character string. The maximum length is 8,000 characters.
- **Varchar(n):** This is for storing a variable-length character string. The maximum length is 8,000 characters.
- **Varchar(max):** This is for storing a variable-length character string. The maximum length is 1,073,741,824 characters.
- **Text:** This is for storing a variable-length character string. The maximum amount is 2 GB of data in the text.

Unicode Strings

- **Nchar(n):** This is for storing fixed-length Unicode data. The maximum length is 4,000 characters.
- **Nvarchar(n):** This is for storing variable-length Unicode data. The maximum length is 4,000 characters.
- **Nvarchar(max):** This is for storing variable-length Unicode data. The maximum length is 536,870,912 characters.

- **Ntext:** This is for storing variable-length Unicode data. The maximum amount is 2 GB of text data.

Binary Data Types

- **Bit:** This allows 0, 1, or NULL.
- **Binary(n):** This is for storing fixed-length binary data. The maximum is 8,000 bytes.
- **Varbinary(n):** This is for storing variable-length binary data. The maximum is 8,000 bytes.
- **Varbinary(max):** This is for storing variable-length binary data. The maximum is 2 GB.
- **Image:** This is for storing variable-length binary data. The maximum is 2 GB.

Numeric Data Types

- **Tinyint:** This allows 0–255 numbers to be stored. The storage is 1 byte.
- **Smallint:** This allows numbers to be stored between -32,768 and 32,767. The storage is 2 bytes.
- **Int:** This allows whole numbers between -2,147,483,648 and 2,147,483,647. The storage is 4 bytes.
- **Bigint:** This allows numbers between -9,223,372,036,854,775,808 and

88

9,223,372,036,854,775,807 to be stored. The storage is 8 bytes.

- **Decimal(p,s):** This is for storing fixed precision and scale numbers. It allows numbers from -10^38 +1 to 10^38 -1 to be stored. The p parameter will indicate the digits of the maximum amount that can be stored in total. This contains both numbers to the right and left of a decimal point. A value between 1 and 38 should be assigned for the p parameter. The default is 18. The maximum amount of digits and how many can be stored to the right of the decimal point will be indicated by the s parameter. The s must be of a value of 0 to the p. 0 is the default. The storage is 5-17 bytes.
- **Numeric(p,s):** This is for fixed precision and scale numbers. It allows numbers between -10^38 +1 to 10^38 -1. The p parameter will indicate the maximum number of digits that can be stored in total. This contains both the numbers left and right of the decimal point. The p must be a value between 1 and 38. The default is 18. The s parameter will indicate many digits to be stored to the right of the decimal point. The s must be a value of 0 to the p. The default is 0. The storage is 5-17 bytes.
- **Smallmoney:** This is for storing monetary data between -214,748.3648 to 214,748.3647. The storage is 4 bytes.

- **Money:** This is for storing monetary data between -922,337,203,685,477.5808 to 922,337,203,685,477.5807. The storage is 8 bytes.
- **Float(n):** This is for storing a floating precision number from -1.79E + 308 to 1.79E + 308. Whether the field should hold either 4 or 8 bytes will be indicated by the n parameter. Float (24) holds a field of 4 bytes, while float(53) holds a field of 8 bytes. 53 is the default value of the n parameter. The storage will be between 4 and 8 bytes.
- **Real:** This is for storing a number of floating precision between -3.40E + 38 and 3.40E + 38. The storage is 4 bytes.

Date/Time Data Types

- **Datetime:** This is for storing a date anywhere between January 1, 1753, and December 31, 9999. This has an accuracy of 3.33 milliseconds. The storage is 8 bytes.
- **Datetime2:** This is to store a date anywhere between January 1, 0001, and December 31, 9999. 100 nanoseconds are its accuracy. The storage is 6 to 8 bytes.
- **Smalldatetime:** This is to store a date anywhere between January 1, 1900, and June 6, 2079. One minute is its accuracy. The storage is 4 bytes.

- **Date:** This is for storing only a date (Any date between January 1, 0001, and December 31, 9999). The storage is 3 bytes.
- **Time:** This is for storing only time. 100 nanoseconds are its accuracy. The storage is between 3 to 5 bytes.
- **Datetimeoffset:** With the addition of a time zone offset, datetime2 is the same thing. The storage is between 8 and 10 bytes.
- **Timestamp:** Every time that a row is either created or modified, this will store a unique number. The timestamp is based on an internal clock and won't correspond with real-time. Each table may only have one timestamp variable.

Other Data Types

- **Sql_variant:** This stores 8,000 bytes of different data types. The only data types that it will not store are text, ntext, and timestamp.
- **Unique identifier:** This is also known as (GUID), and it will store a globally unique identifier.
- **XML:** This stores data formatted in XML. Its max is 2 GB.
- **Cursor:** Database operations use this to store a reference.

- **Table:** For later processing, this stores result set information.

Chapter 5: Types of Symbols Used

Before you can construct or create proper and correct SQL statements or queries, you have to be familiar with the most commonly used symbols in SQL.

SQL symbols

Semicolon ;

This is used to end SQL statements or queries. It should always be added to complete the query. An exception is that of the Cache's SQL, which does not use semicolons.

Open and Close Parentheses ( )

These have several uses. Those are used to enclose data types, conditions, and sometimes names of columns.

They are too used to enclose a subquery in the "from" clause and arithmetic equations. Also, when there are varied values and comma-separated data.

Double Quotes " "

These indicate a delimited identifier or values.

Single Quotes ' '

This is usually used to enclose "strings" of data types or conditions.

Asterisk *

The asterisk indicates "all" data, columns, or tables.

Underscore _

This is used in table or column names to identify them properly. It is also used as an identifier.

Percent %

This is used as an identifier name for the first characters of your data, such as data names, system variables, and keywords.

Comma ,

This symbol is used as a list separator such as, in a series of columns or multiple field names.

Open and Close Square Brackets [ ]

This is used to enclose a list of match data types, or characters, or pattern strings.

Plus +

This is usually used in number operations.

There are still various symbols that you can learn as your knowledge advances.

These common symbols are appropriate for a beginner who is just starting to learn SQL.

Chapter 6: SQL Triggers

Triggers in SQL are used to automatically perform an action on a database when DDL or DML operation takes place.

For example, picture a situation where you want to give a discount of 10% on the prices of all the examination records that will be inserted in the future; you can do so using triggers.

Another example can be log maintenance. You want that whenever a new record is inserted, entry is made in the log table as well.

You can perform such operations with triggers. There are 2 types of triggers in SQL: AFTER and INSTEAD OF triggers.

The AFTER trigger is executed after an action has been performed.

For instance, if you want to log the operation after an operation has been performed, you can use the AFTER trigger.

On the other hand, if you want to perform a different operation in place of the actual event, you can use the INSTEAD OF trigger.

In this chapter, we shall see an example of both types of triggers.

Trigger Syntax

Trigger syntax is complex, therefore before seeing an actual example, let's first understand the syntax. Take a look at the following script:

CREATE [OR ALTER] TRIGGER [schema_name.]name_of_trigger

ON {TABLE | VIEW }

{ FOR | AFTER | INSTEAD OF }

{ [INSERT] [,] [UPDATE] [,] [DELETE] }

AS

{

BEGIN

The SQL statements to execute ....

END

}

Now let's see what is happening in the above script, line by line.

To create a trigger, the CREATE TRIGGER statement is used.

To ALTER existing trigger, we can use ALTER TRIGGER statement.

Next, the database scheme and the name of the trigger are specified.

After that, the ON TABLE clause specifies the name of the table or view.

Next, you have to mention the type of trigger using FOR clause.

Here you can write AFTER or INSTEAD OF.

Finally, you write AS BEGIN and END statements.

Inside the BEGIN and END clause, you write the SQL statements that you want to be executed when the trigger fires.

AFTER Trigger

Now let's see a simple example of AFTER trigger.

We will insert a new record in the Patients table of the Hospital database.

When the record is inserted, we will use an AFTER trigger to add an entry into the Patient_Logs table.

We do not have the Patient_Logs table at the moment in the Hospital database.

Execute the following query to create this table:

USE Hospital;

CREATE TABLE Patient_Logs

(

id INT IDENTITY(1,1) PRIMARY KEY,

patient_id INT NOT NULL,

patient_name VARCHAR(50) NOT NULL,

action_performed VARCHAR(50) NOT NULL

)

Now we have our Patient_Logs table.

Let's create the AFTER trigger that will automatically log an entry in the Patient_Logs table whenever a record is inserted Patients table.

Take a look at the following script:

USE Hospital;

GO - begin a new batch

CREATE TRIGGER [dbo].[PATIENT_TRIGGER]

ON [dbo].[Patients]

AFTER INSERT

AS

BEGIN

    SET NOCOUNT ON;

    DECLARE @patient_id INT, @patient_nameVARCHAR(50)

SELECT @patient_id = INSERTED.id, @patient_name = INSERTED.name

FROM INSERTED

INSERT INTO Patient_Logs

VALUES(@patient_id, @patient_name, "Insert Operation")

END

Here in the above script, we create a trigger named PATIENT_TRIGGER on dbo database scheme.

This is AFTER type trigger and fires whenever a new record is inserted into the Patients table.

In the body of the trigger starting from BEGIN, we declared set a variable NOCOUNT ON.

This returns the number of affected rows.

Next, we declared 2 variables @patient_id and @patient_name.

These variables will hold the id and name of the newly inserted patient record.

The INSERTED clause here is a temporary table that holds a newly inserted record.

The SELECT statement is used in the script to select the id and name from the INSERTED table and store them in patient_id and patient_name variables, respectively.

Finally, the INSERT statement is used to insert the values in these variables to the Patient_Logs table.

Now, simply insert a new record in the Patients table by executing the following query:

USE Hospital

INSERT INTO Patients

VALUES("Suzana," 28, "Male," "AB-," 65821479)

When the above query executes, the PATIENT_TRIGGER fires, which inserts a record in the Patient_Logs table too.

Now, if you select records from your Patient_logs table, you will see your new log entry.

USE Hospital

SELECT * FROM Patient_Logs

The output will look like this:

id	patient_id	patient_name	action_performed
1	14	Suzana	Insert Operation

INSTEAD OF Trigger

We have already created an AFTER trigger, which is executed after an event has occurred.

In this section, we will study INSTEAD OF triggers.

The INSTEAD OF trigger executes when we want to execute an alternative action instead of executing the event that triggered the action.

For instance, consider a scenario where you want to update the price of different examinations.

You also want to implement the condition that if the price is less than 250, it should not be updated.

Also, you want to keep track of all the efforts to update the price.

In such a case, you can use the INSTEAD OF trigger to execute a script that checks. If the updated price is less than 250 you, log entry into the table that "price cannot be updated," otherwise update the price and log the entry that "price updated."

Chapter 7: Using VIEWS in SQL

VIEWS are virtual tables or stored SQL queries in the databases that have predefined queries and unique names. They are the resulting tables from your SQL queries. As a beginner, you may want to learn about how you can use VIEWS. Among their numerous uses is their flexibility can combine rows and columns from VIEWS.

Here are important pointers and advantages in using VIEWS:

- You can summarize data from different tables or a subset of columns from various tables.
- You can control what users of your databases can see, and restrict what you don't want them to view.
- You can organize your database for your user's easy manipulation, while simultaneously protecting your non-public files.
- You can modify, or edit, or UPDATE your data. Sometimes there are limitations, though, such as being able to access only one column when using VIEW.
- You can create columns from various tables for your reports.

- You can increase the security of your databases because VIEWS can display only the information that you want to be displayed.
- You can protect specific information from other users.
- You can provide easy and efficient accessibility or access paths to your data to users.
- You can allow users of your databases to derive various tables from your data without dealing with the complexity of your databases.
- You can rename columns through views.
- If you are a website owner, VIEWS can also provide domain support.
- The WHERE clause in the SQL VIEWS query may not contain subqueries.
- For the INSERT keyword to function, you must include all NOT NULL columns from the original table.
- Do not use the WITH ENCRYPTION (unless utterly necessary) clause for your VIEWS because you may not be able to retrieve the SQL.
- Avoid creating VIEWS for each base table (original table).
- This can add more workload in managing your databases.
- As long as you create your base SQL query properly, there is no need to create VIEWS for each base table.

- VIEWS that uses the DISTINCT and ORDER BY clauses or keywords may not produce the expected results.
- VIEWS can be updated under the condition that the SELECT clause may not contain the summary functions; and/or the set operators, and the set functions.
- When UPDATING, there should be a synchronization of your base table with your VIEWS table.
- Therefore, you must analyze the VIEW table, so that the data presented are still correct, each time you UPDATE the base table.
- Avoid creating VIEWS that are unnecessary because this will clutter your catalog.
- Specify "column_names" clearly.
- The FROM clause of the SQL VIEWS query may not contain many tables unless specified.
- The SQL VIEWS query may not contain HAVING or GROUP BY.
- The SELECT keyword can join your VIEW table with your base table.

How to Create VIEWS

You can create VIEWS through the following easy steps:

Step 1: Check if your system is appropriate to implement VIEW queries.

Step 2: Make use of the CREATE VIEW SQL statement.

Step 3: Use keywords for your SQL syntax just like with any other SQL main queries.

Step 4: Your basic CREATE VIEW statement or syntax will appear like this:

Example: CREATE VIEW "table_Name"_VIEW AS

SELECT"column_name1"

FROM"table_name"

WHERE [condition];

Let's have a specific example based on our original table.

Employees Salary

Names	Age	Salary	City
Williams, Michael	22	30000.00	Casper
Colton, Jean	24	37000.00	San Diego

Anderson, Ted	30	45000.00	Laramie
Dixon, Allan	27	43000.00	Chicago
Clarkson, Tim	25	35000.00	New York
Alaina, Ann	32	41000.00	Ottawa
Rogers, David	29	50000.00	San Francisco
Lambert, Jancy	38	47000.00	Los Angeles
Kennedy, Tom	27	34000.00	Denver
Schultz, Diana	40	46000.00	New York

Based on the table above, you may want to create a view of the customer's names and the City only.

This is how you should write your statement.

Example: CREATE VIEW EmployeesSalary_VIEW AS

SELECT Names, City

FROM EmployeesSalary;

From the resulting VIEW table, you can now create a query such as a statement below.

SELECT * FROM EmployeesSalary_VIEW;

This SQL query will display a table that will appear this way:

Employees Salary

Names	City
Williams, Michael	Casper
Colton, Jean	San Diego
Anderson, Ted	Laramie
Dixon, Allan	Chicago
Clarkson, Tim	New York
Alaina, Ann	Ottawa
Rogers, David	San Francisco
Lambert, Jancy	Los Angeles
Kennedy, Tom	Denver
Schultz, Diana	New York

Using the Keyword WITH CHECK OPTION

These keywords ascertain that there will be no return errors with the INSERT and UPDATE returns and that all conditions are fulfilled properly.

Example: CREATE VIEW "table_Name"_VIEW AS

SELECT

"column_name1","column_name2"

FROM "table_name"

WHERE [condition]

WITH CHECK OPTION;

Applying this SQL statement to the same conditions (display name and city), we can come up now with our WITH CHECK OPTION statement.

Example: CREATE VIEW EmployeesSalary_VIEW AS

SELECT Names, City

FROM EmployeesSalary

WHERE City IS NOT NULL

WITH CHECK OPTION;

The SQL query above will ensure that there will be no NULL returns in your resulting table.

Dropping VIEWS

You can drop your VIEWS whenever you don't need them anymore.

The SQL syntax is the same as the main SQL statements.

>Example: DROP VIEW EmployeesSalary_VIEW;

Updating VIEWS

You can easily UPDATE VIEWS by following the SQL query for the main queries.

Example: CREATE OR REPLACE VIEW "tablename"_VIEWS(could also be VIEWS_"tablename") AS

>SELECT "column_name"
>
>FROM "table_name"
>
>WHERE condition;

Deleting VIEWS

The SQL syntax for DELETING VIEWS is much the same way as DELETING DATA using the main SQL query.

The difference only is in the name of the table.

If you use the VIEW table example above and want to delete the City column, you can come up with this SQL statement.

Example: DELETE FROM EmployeesSalary_VIEW

       WHERE City ='New York';

The SQL statement above would have this output:

Employees Salary

Names	Age	Salary	City
Williams, Michael	22	30000.00	Casper
Colton, Jean	24	37000.00	San Diego
Anderson, Ted	30	45000.00	Laramie
Dixon, Allan	27	43000.00	Chicago
Alaina, Ann	32	41000.00	Ottawa
Rogers, David	29	50000.00	San Francisco
Lambert, Jancy	38	47000.00	Los Angeles
Kennedy, Tom	27	34000.00	Denver

Inserting Rows

Creating an SQL in INSERTING ROWS is similar to the UPDATING VIEWS syntax.

Make sure you have included the NOT NULL columns.

Example: INSERT INTO"table_name"_VIEWS "column_name1"

WHERE value1;

VIEWS can be utterly useful if you utilize them appropriately.

Chapter 8: Using Operators to Categorize Information

When we are talking about operators in your database, we are talking about the reserved characters and words that are mostly used in the WHERE clause of your statements.

Operators are used to performing operations in your statements, such as mathematical equations and comparisons, and they can even help to specify the parameters you want to set for the statements.

And of course, they can connect more than one parameter that is found within the SQL statement.

There are a few different types of operators that you will be able to use within your SQL statement including:

- Arithmetic operators
- Comparison operators
- Logical operators
- Operators for negating conditions

Each of these will work in a slightly different way to help you to get the results that you want.

Logical Operators

The logical operators are going to be the keywords that you will use in your statements to perform comparisons.

Some of the logical operators you can use include:

- **In:** This operator will allow you to compare the value of specified literal values that are set. You will get a true if one or more of the specified values is equal to the value that you test.
- **Like:** The like operator is going to make it so that you can compare a value against others that are similar. You will usually combine it with the "_" or the "%" sign to get more done. The underscore is used to represent a number or a character ad the % is used for several characters, zero, or one.
- **Unique:** With the unique operator, you will be able to take a look at one or more of your data rows and see if they are unique or not.
- **Exists:** You will need to use this operator to find the data rows that will meet the criteria that you put down. It

allows you to put down some criteria and see if any rows exist that meet with this.

- **Between:** You can use this operator to find values that will fall into a specific range. You will need to assign the maximum and the minimum values to make this work.
- **Is null:** The is null operator will allow you to compare the value of your choosing with a NULL one.
- **Any and all:** Any and all values often go together. Any operator is going to compare a value against all of the values on a list. The list of values is to be set up with predetermined conditions. All, on the other hand, will compare the values that you select against the values that are in a different value set.

These are important for helping you to look up new data points within your database or to make some comparisons.

You can try out a few of these in your database and see what they come up with.

Comparison Operators

The comparison operators are great if you would like to check the single values that are found inside of an SQL statement.

This particular category is going to be composed of some basic mathematical signs, so they are pretty easy to figure out.

Some of the comparison operators that you will be able to use within your SQL database includes:

- **Non-equality:** If you are testing the non-equality operator, you will use the "<>" signs. The operation is going to give you the result of TRUE if the data does not equal and FALSE if the data does equal. You can also use the "!=" to check for this as well.
- **Equality:** You will be able to use this operator to test out some single values in your statement. You will simply need to use the "=" sign to check for this. You are only going to get a response if the data that you chose has identical values. If the values aren't equal, you will get a false, and if they are equal, you will get a true.
- **Greater:** Than values and Less-than values—these 2 are going to rely on the "<" and ">" signs to help you out. They will work as stand-alone operators if you would like, but often they are more effective when you combine them with some of the other operators.

Arithmetic Operations

These operators are great if you are looking to do some mathematical operations in your SQL language.

There are 4 main type types that you will be able to use in your equations.

These include:

- **Addition:** You will just need to use the "+" sign to get started on using addition. For this example, we are going to add up the values for the overhead column and the materials column.

    The statement that works for this is:

    SELECT MATERIALS + OVERHEAD FROM PRODUCTION_COST_TBL.

- **Subtraction:** You can also do some basic subtraction when it comes to your SQL statements. You will simply need to use the "-" sign to do this.
- **Multiplication:** It is possible to do multiplication from your tables as well. You would need to use the "*" sign to do this.

- **Division:** This one will just need the "/" sign to get started.

You can combine a few of the arithmetic operations as well if this is what your process needs.

For example, you may want to go through and figure out how much you are earning each month and then subtract the costs when you are all done.

Your earnings are probably going to have more than one entry, and this is possible for how much you spent as well, so you may need to do a few different operations to make this happen.

If you are going to use any combination of arithmetic operators, you need to remember that the principles of precedence are going to come into play.

This means that the syntax is going to take care of all the things that need to be multiplied first, and then the division, and then addition, and then subtraction.

It will not go from left to right, but it will go around to work with the symbols that you have up for the arithmetic operations, so keep this in mind when you are writing out your syntax.

Operators to Use When Negating Conditions

In some cases, you will want to negate the operators in your database when you want to change the viewpoint of the condition.

You will want to use the NOT command to cancel the operator that it is used for.

Some of the techniques that you can use to do this include:

Not equal: You can use this when you want to find results that are not equal to something. For example, if you did use the "<>" or the "!=" symbols, you would get anything that was not equal to the value that you placed into the equation.

Not between: You can also negate with the not between and the between operators. For example, if you are using a price, you could decide that you want to find the values that are not between 500 and 1000 or any value. This means that all the values that come up need to be either 499 and below or 1001 and above.

Not in: If you will be able to use the not in command to negate the in operator. You will be able to pick some values that you don't want to have listed, and then the not in command will return you anything that doesn't fit in that amount.

Not like: This is the term that you will use to negate the operator. When you are using this, you are only going to see the values that are different from the ones that you placed into the equation.

Is not null: This one will work to negate the is null command. You will want to use this to check for the data that isn't null.

These are going to help you to set up some of the conditions of your search, so you can get a wide variety of information back without having to go through every little part of your database.

Conjunctive Operators

There are going to be times when you will need to use several different criteria to make something happen.

For example, if you are getting some results that are confusing from the database searches, you may decide to add in a few different criteria to see how it will turn up.

You will be able to combine some different criteria in the statement to make the conjunctive operator.

Some of the conjunctive operators that you can use include:

- **OR:** You will use this statement to combine the conditions of the WHERE clause. Before this statement can take action, the criteria need to be separated by the OR, or it should be TRUE.
- **AND:** This operator is going to make it easier to include multiple criteria into the WHERE section of your statement. The statement will then only take action when the criteria have been segregated by the AND, and they are all true.

Keep in mind there are times when you will want to combine these operators inside of the statement.

Just make sure that you are adding in parentheses to improve readability.

Chapter 9: Users and Roles

One of the things that we will need to focus on when we are handling some of our databases and what we can do with all of this is to look at who is allowed to gain access to the database, what each person on the database is allowed to do, and so on.

If you have a large database that your customers can get onto, you likely want to go through and set up some limitations, for example, so that they are not able to make major changes to what is on the database overall.

This chapter is going to take some time to look at the users and the roles of your database, and how you can get these set up for some of your own needs as well.

Logins to the Server

The first thing that we will take a look at is how we can log in to one of our servers with SQL.

You can do this with the help of the command prompt on your computer, or by use of any of the graphical management tools that you have.

When you do go through and log into an SQL server instance using the administration tools, though, you are going to be prompted to answer a few things like adding in the server name, the login for the SQL Server, and a password.

You can also go through and log into this with the help of Windows Authentication.

With this option, you will not need to provide this information each time that you get onto the server because you can use the information from your Windows account to do this automatically.

If your server is running in the authentication for mixed-mode, and you log in with the SQL Server Authentication, then you have to work with the password and log in as we talked about before.

It is usually suggested that you work with Windows Authentication if possible.

Sometimes when you go through this process, you will need to spend some time verifying the connection protocol that you have.

When you do connect over to the Database Engine, you will need to go through and work with some queries to help check out the current connection and to ensure that you are going to get the authentication method.

If you use this query well, you will be able to tell if the connection you are using is encrypted or not.

SELECT net_transport, auth_scheme, encrypt_option

FROM sys.dm_exec_connections

WHERE session_id = @@SPID;

And that is all that you need to do to make sure that you can log into your SQL database.

If you spend time looking over the Windows Authentication, the process is even easier because you can be logged in automatically if you are already using your Windows account, but the other options are going to be important to all of this as well and will work out if you choose to go with them as well.

Assigning Roles in the Database

We need to make sure that we take some time to assign roles in the database.

Some people should just get the most basic access to the database, and then some who are going to be in control of running the database and making changes.

And there are often a lot of different things that show up in between when it comes to the roles and the access points of the people who can be on that database.

You can spend some time grouping privileges in the database roles with the help of Oracle.

An object owner can create a given role and then grant that over when needed.

For example, maybe you are an administrator for a database for a big retailer.

Each day, there is the hiring of some new store clerks.

The usage of your database at the time is going to allow them the option of doing a dozen different requirements, and these can include:

- INSERT into the table for sales.
- UPDATE table for inventory when it is needed.
- DELETE from the table of orders as well.

There are going to be a few roles that are already created and set up when it is in the database, which is going to make it easier to manage some of the tasks that are out there.

You can choose to add in some more if you would like along the way, but these are the basics that will make it easier if you are just looking for something to get started with along the way.

Some of the given roles that Oracle is going to supply to you on the first installation of the database will include:

- **Connect:** This is going to include all of the privileges that are needed to ensure that someone can connect with that database.
- **Resource**: This one is going to include several roles that a developer can use to help in creating and managing a given application, for instance, altering and creating several objects, with the inclusion of tables, sequences, and views.
- **Recovery_catalog_owner:** This is going to allow the grantee to come through and administer the catalog for Oracle Recovery Manager.
- **Scheduler_Admin:** This one is going to allow the grantee the option to manage the Oracle job scheduler.

- **DBA:** This one is going to help provide a user with several of the core privileges that are required to help administer the database. These can manage the users, the security, the space, the parameters of the system, and even some of the backups that should happen as well.

As the administrator of your database, you need to consider what kinds of access you would like to assign to the different people who are going to get onto your system.

The decisions that you make will often depend on the information that is going to be found on the database, and even some of the different people who you think will be there as well.

This will make it easier to have more control over the database and who can access it, make changes, and more.

Commands to Help With Users and Roles

With some of this in mind, we are going to spend a moment to look at a few more of the commands that we have not had the time to look over yet in this guidebook.

These commands are going to help you with some of the different user roles and more that you have, and some of the other administrative tasks that you would want to focus your attention on here as well.

Some of the other options that we need to spend our time here will include:

- **LIKE:** This is going to be the special operator that we can use along with the WHERE clause. It is a good one to help us find the specific patterns that are going to show up in our column.
- **AVG:** This is the command that we are going to use when we want to make sure that we can get the average function for any of our columns that are numeric at the time.
- **ROUND:** This is going to be a type of function that can take the name of the column as an integer as the arguments. It is going to round the values in the column to the number of decimal places that are specified by the integer.
- **SUM:** Then, we can move on to the SUM function. This one is going to be able to take its argument from the name of the column and then will allow us to return the sum of all of the values that we can find in that column.
- **MAX:** This one is going to be the function that can take the name of a column and use that as its argument. It is

then able to return the largest value to this column, as well.

- **MIN:** This is the final function that we are going to take a look at, and it is going to help us take the name of a column as the main argument that we want to work with and then will return the smallest value that is in that column at the time.

Chapter 10: Normalizing Your Database

When we are talking about SQL, normalization is the process of taking your database and breaking it up into some smaller units.

Developers will often use this procedure as a way to make your database easier to organize and manage.

Some databases are really large and hard to handle.

If you have thousands of customers, for example, your database could get quite large.

This will make it difficult to get through all the information at times because there is just so much that you will have to filter through to get what you want.

But with database normalization, this is not as big of an issue.

The developer will be able to split up some of the information so that the search engine is better able to go through the database without taking so long or running into as many issues.

Also, going through with database normalization will help to ensure the accuracy and integrity of all the information that you place into the database.

How Do I Normalize the Database?

Now that you know some of the reasons for choosing to do database normalization, it is time to work on doing the actual process.

The process of normalization means that you are going to decrease any of the redundancies that are inside the database.

You will be able to use this technique any time that you want to design or even redesign your database.

Some of the tools that you need and the processes that you should learn to make this happen will include:

Raw Databases

Any database that hasn't gone through the process of normalization can contain tables that have the same information inside of it.

This redundant information can slow down the search process and can make it hard for your database to find the information that you want.

Some of the security issues that you could have with a database that hasn't gone through normalization include slow queries, inefficient database updates, and poor security.

This is all because you have the same information in there a few times, and you have divided it into smaller pieces to make things easier on your search.

Below is an example of a database that will need some help with normalization.

```
COMPANY_DATABASE

emp_id              cust_id
last_name           cust_name
first_name          cust_address
middle_name         cust_city
address             cust_state
city                cust_zip
state               cust_phone
zip                 cust_fax
phone               ord_num
pager               qtu
position            Ord_date
date_hire           prod_id
pay_rate            prod_desc
bonus               cost
date_last_raise
```

As you can see, there are quite a few points where the same information is asked several times.

And while this is a small table, some of the bigger ones could have more issues that will slow down the results and end up in a mess.

Using the process of normalization on your original database can ensure that you are going to cut out some of this mess and make things better for the user and for yourself to find the information needed.

Logical Design

Each of the databases that you are working on needs to be created as well as designed with the end-users in mind.

You can make a fantastic database, but if the users find that it is difficult to navigate, you have just wasted a lot of time in the process.

A logical model, or logical design, is a process where you are going to be able to do this because you have arranged the data into smaller groups that are easy for the user to find and work with.

When you are creating the data groups, you must remember that they should be manageable, organized, and logical.

Logical design is going to make it easier for you to reduce, and in some cases even eliminate, any of the data repetition that goes on in your database.

What Are the Needs of the End-User?

When you are designing your database, it is important to keep the end-users needs in mind.

The end-users are the ones who will be using the database that you develop, so you will need to keep some of your personal feelings out of this and just concentrate on picking out a way to work the database that is beneficial to the customer.

In general, you will want to create a user-friendly database, and if you can add an intuitive interface, this can be great too.

Good visuals are a way to attract the customer, but you need to have excellent performance present as well, or the customer may get frustrated with what you are trying to sell them on the page.

When you are working on creating a new database for your business, some of the questions that you should answer to ensure that you are making the right database for your customers include:

- What data will I store here?
- How will the users be able to access the data?
- Do the users need any special privileges to access the data?

- How can the users" group the data within the database?
- What connection will I make between the data pieces that I will store?
- I will ensure the integrity and accuracy of the data.

Data Repetition

When creating your database, you need to make sure that the data is not repetitive.

You need to work to minimize this redundancy as much as possible.

For example, if you have the customer's name in more than one table, you are wasting a lot of time and space in the process because this duplicated data is going to lead to inefficient use of your storage space.

Outside of wasting the storage space, this repetitive entry will lead to confusion.

This is going to happen when the data in one of the tables don't match up with a different one, even when the tables were created for the same person or object.

Normal Forms

A normal form will be a method of identifying the levels or the depth that you will need to normalize the database.

In some cases, it just needs to be cleaned up a little bit, but other times you will have a lot of work ahead of you to make that table look nice.

When you are using the normal form, you are going to determine what level of normalization you need to perform on the database.

There are 3 forms that you will use for normalizing the databases, including the first form, the second form, and the third form.

Every subsequent form that you use will rely on the techniques that you used on the form before it.

With this, you need to have it in the right form before you can move on.

For example, you are not able to skip from the first form to the third form without doing the second form there as well.

- **First form:** The goal of using this form is to take the data and segregate it into tables. Once the tables are designed, the user will be able to assign a primary key to either some or each of the tables. To attain this first form, you will divide up the data into small units, and each one needs to have 2 things; a primary key and also be free from any redundant data.
- **The second form:** The goal of using the second form is to find the data that is at least partially reliant on those primary keys. Then this data can be transferred over to a new table as well. This will help to sort out the important information and will leave behind redundant information or other things that you don't need.
- **The third form:** The goal of the third form is to eliminate the information that does not depend on any of your primary keys. This will help to get rid of the information that is in the way and slowing down the computer and will ensure that you are getting rid of the redundant and unneeded information along the way.

Naming Conventions

When you are working on the normalization process, it is a good idea to worry about the naming conventions.

You will need to use the names to store and then later retrieve your data.

You should pick out names that are relevant in some way to the information that you are working on so that it is easier to remember these names later on.

This will help to avoid confusion and keep things organized in the database.

Benefits of Normalizing Your Database

We have spent some time talking about normalization in your database so far in this guidebook, but what are the benefits?

Why should you go through this whole process simply to clean out the database that your customers are using?

Wouldn't it works out just fine to leave the information and let the search figure it out regardless of the redundancies and other information that you don't need?

There are many benefits to doing this process including:

- Keeping the database organized and easier to use
- Reducing repetitive information that could come up

- Better security for the whole system so you can protect your users better than before.
- Better flexibility on the design that you have for the database
- Great consistency within the database.

It may seem like a hassle to go through and normalize the database, but it makes the whole experience better.

Your customers will have a better time finding the information that they want, the searching and purchasing process will become more streamlined, and your security will be top of the line.

One thing to keep in mind, though is that, there is a downside to using normalization.

This process does reduce the performance of the database in some cases.

A normalized database is going to need more input/output, processing power, and memory to get the work done.

Once normalized, your database is going to need to merge data and find the required tables to get anything done.

While this can help to make the database system more effective, it is still important to realize that there are some downsides.

Denormalization

Another process that you may wish to learn about is denormalization.

This allows you to take a normalized database and change it so that the database can accept repetition.

This is going to be used in some cases to increase how well the database can perform.

While there are some benefits to using the normalization process, it is going to slow down the system of the database simply because it is working through so many automated functions.

Depending on the case, it could be better to have this redundant information rather than working with a slow system.

The normalization of your database has many great benefits, and it is pretty easy to set it all up.

You just need to teach the database to get rid of information that it finds repetitive, or that could be causing some of the issues within your system.

This can help to provide more consistency, flexibility, and security on the whole system.

Chapter 11: The Security of Databases

Databases are containers that maintain all kinds of data, corporate secrets, employee data that is sensitive, lists of employees scheduled for separation, and many other types of information that need proper security and access control.

Many companies today are using Microsoft's active directory to manage users and sort them into access profiles using a group policy process.

How this works in practice is that employees of a company are assigned group permissions based on their job title, and within those group permissions, more individualized permissions are created depending on employee rank within a group.

SQL does interact with Active Directory for access control, but it does not provide internal security regarding authorization.

The SQL application itself provides these services.

There are 4 main components of database security: authentication, authorization, encryption, and access control.

Authentication pertains to validating whether a user has permission to access any resources of the system.

The most common method of authentication by far is the username and password, verifying the credentials of a potential user.

Single sign-on systems also exist which use certificate authentication that the user does not interact with directly.

The end user's system is prepared with information that provides authentication automatically without prompt.

Corporations go to great lengths to ensure system access is authenticated and appropriately authorized.

Encryption strengthens this access control by scrambling data into indecipherable gibberish to any potential interceptors of transmitted data.

Microsoft SQL Server uses RSA encryption to protect data.

RSA is a data encryption algorithm that uses a layered hierarchical structure along with key management to secure data.

Authorization is the process that determines what resources within a system an authenticated user access.

Once a client has provided acceptable credentials, the next step is to decide which entities the subject has permission to access or modify.

Lastly, SQL uses change tracking to maintain a log of all the actions of potentially unauthorized users.

It is also possible to track the activities of all authorized users, but that isn't a part of the security functionality of change tracking.

Power-users or super-users with elevated permissions may have access to all systems, but that does not authorize them as users of the database.

Tracking changes protect a system from operations performed by users with elevated credentials.

SQL uses a security model comprised of 3 classes that interplay with each other:

- Principals have permission to access specific objects.
- Securable refer to resources within a database that the system regulates access to.
- Permission is the right to view, edit, or delete securable, and this access is pre-defined.

This security model belongs primarily to the Microsoft SQL Server, but there are equivalents within other SQL management products such as MySQL, DB2, or 11G.

The theories behind modeling access control are widespread across the IT industry and cover much more than database security.

These same principals are behind nearly all enterprise applications that house sensitive data.

Security is a profound subject, and there are comprehensive books available on securing enterprise resources.

The goal of this chapter is to focus on the most relevant topics after providing a brief overview of the general landscape of database security.

The primary elements covered briefly above are an excellent base to expand upon the ideas of access roles and schema related to security.

Microsoft defines schema as "A collection of database objects that are owned by a single person and form a single namespace."

The single namespace refers to a limitation that does not allow 2 tables in the same schema to have the same name.

Data consistency and referential ease are the guiding ideas behind SQL's design, and this is the reason behind the limitation.

Principals can be a single user or single login as well as a group principle.

Multiple users sharing one role are grouped using group policies, and all can cooperatively own a schema or many schemas.

Transferring schema from one principle to another is possible and does not require renaming unless the new owner maintains a schema that would create a duplicate name.

There are T-SQL statements for managing schema, but a majority of this work belongs to database administrators, not the principles of a database.

Roles are another layer of security for identifying access dependent upon title and responsibilities.

There are many different kinds of roles available. SQL comes with fixed server roles and fixed database roles that provide implicit permissions. It is also possible to create customized application roles, user-defined server roles, and user-defined database roles.

Microsoft's Fixed Server Roles

Roles are very important to database security.

All the other security functions are built on top of roles.

- **Authentication** determines who can access databases; authorization determines which principles have access to which schema.
- **Encryption** protects data from interception from those external to the company, as well as potential hazards internally. Sensitive data that leaks internally or is

intercepted unintentionally is more dangerous than external threats.

Roles maintain the minutiae of which users are allowed to perform any given operation within a database.

Microsoft teaches security principles that provide a user with the least amount of access possible to perform their duties.

This theory prevents users from having access to resources that they are not trained to use. The same guiding ideas are used with SQL.

The purpose of roles is to limit the amount of access an employee has to a database that does not pertain to their specific responsibilities within the schema.

Owners are considered "sysadmins," but all other users of a database have specialized functions based on their training and experience.

Database administrators are usually part of the IT department, but database owners are rarely within the same department as the database administrators, and so there is a level of autonomy that is necessary because administrators are responsible for maintaining the structure and consistency of dozens and even hundreds of databases.

These rules and roles are all for the end goal of keeping consistent and referential data.

TOP Clause

The TOP clause is typically used for outputting the first N records or a specific percentage of records from a table.

However, variations of this clause may be supported.

For instance, there is a LIMIT clause in MySQL, which is used to fetch a limited number of records from a table.

On the other hand, Oracle supports the ROWNUM command for the same functionality.

The syntax for using the TOP clause is shown below for your reference.

SELECT TOP num|percent col_name(s) FROM t_name WHERE [cond];

Here, num/percent is the number or percent of records that you wish to retrieve from the top of the table, starting with the first record, and col_name is the name of the column that needs to be retrieved.

Lastly, cond is the condition specified as part of the WHERE clause to filter the records based on a condition.

A few working examples of the TOP clause have been given below.

Consider the table named CUST with the following data as the table for which all the queries are written.

ID	Name	Age	Salary
98701	Rohan	45	50000.00
98675	Amit	32	37000.00
98706	Shayla	22	42005.00
98718	Mathews	37	12000.00

If you wish to retrieve the first 2 records from the table CUST, then the query for the same is as follows:

SELECT TOP 2 * FROM CUST;

Upon execution, the following result shall be generated.

ID	Name	Age	Salary

98701	Rohan	45	50000.00
98675	Amit	32	37000.00

In case you are using MySQL, the query needs to change slightly, and the new query will look like this:

SELECT * FROM CUST LIMIT 2;

Lastly, if Oracle is being used as the base RDBMS for running these queries, the query will be:

SELECT * FROM CUST WHERE ROWNUM <= 2;

The execution of the last 2 commands will generate the same result as that generated for the TOP clause.

Since we are using MySQL, the TOP clause showed an error, but the LIMIT clause worked as expected.

Also, please note that some DBMSs sort the result in ascending order. This is a default setting and may vary the order of records in the result set.

Chapter 12: Summary of Database Development

Now that we have had some time to take a look at what SQL is all about, and why we are going to see so much when it comes to working with the relational database, it is time for us to dive into some of the steps that we need to follow to start developing our database as well.

There are a lot of parts that need to come together to make this work for us, and we are going to explore those a bit more in this chapter, so let's get started.

The Components of a Database

The first thing that we need to spend our time taking a look at is the components that are going to be found in our database.

The relational database is certainly going to be among the most common of these databases, and you are likely going to spend a good deal of your time looking through this and figuring out how to use them.

That is why we are going to start our journey with a closer look at some of the components of this kind of table over some of the others.

First, we will see that there are some tables found in our database.

The table is going to be the same thing as a record, which is going to be one of the fundamental components of the data.

It is going to be comprised of a set of fields that are going to be the same in every record that you have, such as the name, address, and the product that the customer purchased.

This kind of database is also going to dictate how the tables are going to work. For example, this database is going to control how we can present this data onscreen and how we can organize the output that we have, based on what kind of query we use and more.

Then there will be the rows. You will find that the tables that come in this kind of database are going to look similar to what we see with a spreadsheet in Excel when we diagram them for a visual reference.

The row on each of these tables will represent a sequential value where the value in row 1A, to start with, is going to relate to the values that will show up in all of the other fields that we use in row 1.

In addition to working with the rows, we are also going to see some use of the columns. These are going to be more of the control features, and they will show us a field of data that is going to occur consistently with each of the tables in our database.

For example, you could have a column that has a header for address, name, email, and telephone.

These are going to be the fields of data that we would like to have shown up for all of the records.

Primary keys are going to be the next thing that we need to work with as well. These are going to be kind of like the identification tags for all of the rows of data that you would like to work with.

Each record is going to come with its primary key in this kind of database, and it needs to be unique.

The primary key could be something like a number that we have assigned over to the customer or be a unique kind of identifier, such as their SS number.

These keys are important because they are going to be used as the queries within this database, but will not be used for some of the external databases at all.

And finally, we are going to end with the foreign keys. These are going to allow us to do some manipulation and searches of the data between the primary database table and some of the other databases that are related at the time.

This can help to keep things more organized and allows us to find more of the information that we are looking for throughout more than one table at a time.

The Lifecycle of System Development

Now it is time for us to look at another topic that is going to be important to what we can do with some of these databases, and this is more about the lifecycle that we will need to follow when it comes to developing our system along the way.

There is going to be a cycle that we need to go through time and again to make sure that we are going to set up the database that we need and get it to work, without having to worry about whether it is going to work the way that we want, and without having to waste a lot of time in the process.

You will find that there are some steps that we can take when it is time to work with this process, and if we are careful and go through each of them in the right manner, then our codes and databases are going to work the way that we would like.

Some of the steps that we need to follow when it is time to work on a system development project will include:

Planning

The first step here is going to be all about planning.

In this step, we are going to spend some time discovering, identifying, and defining the scope that we would like to see with the project, and then we are going to decide the course of action that we want to work with, hopefully, to help us address the issues that we would like to be able to solve in this system solution.

This is a very important phase, and we need to spend some time with it because it is going to help set the tone for how successful we can be in this project overall.

This is why, during this phase, we need to focus on doing a thorough amount of research to help us figure out the resources, budget, personnel, technical aspects, and more of the project that we want to handle.

Once we have had some time to take a look at the planning stage, it is time for us to work on the analysis.

The purpose of working through this phase is to help us to better understand the business as well as the processing needs of our project at this time.

In this stage, we are going to see that the development team is going to consider some of the functional requirements of the system to assess how the solution we are coming up with is going to help meet the expectations that are there for the end-user, right from the beginning.

We can figure out the requirements of our end-users, thanks to some of the research that we did before, and we can document these right away.

Then we have to go through a feasibility study to help us to determine if the project is going to be feasible from a financial, organizational, social, or even a more technological standpoint along the way.

Now we are ready to go onto the third phase, which is going to be all about the design.

After we have gone through and done a pretty comprehensive kind of analysis phase, it is time to work on the design phase.

This one is going to take a look at the elements, components, security levels, modules, and more that we need to define for the system and then evaluate how we would like to see this finished system work for our needs, and even how it is going to look like in the end.

This is going to need to be done in a lot of detail to ensure that the system is going to include all of the necessary features to meet the operational and functional aspects of all projects.

Development

Development is next on the list.

We will find that an approved design phase from above is going to be important when we will work with the development of this system.

When we reach this phase, we will find that our development team is going to be hard at work writing out the code and making sure that the system is going to get up and running.

This one is often going to be the most robust of all the other ones because it is going to include all of the labor-intensive efforts and can help us to get the database done.

During this phase, we have to make sure that we test and work on the database a bit, as well.

This ensures that we are positive that the data is going to stay in the database and that it is going to work the way that we would like in the process as well.

We also need to go through and double-check that everything is safe and secure and that we, as well as the customers, are going to be able to rely on the database that we are creating in the process.

Maintenance

And finally, we need to spend some time working on the maintenance of our system.

We can't just put a database up and hope that it is good forever on its own without any help from others or from some maintenance along the way.

You have to take the time to check on the database all of the time, ensuring that we are going to see some of the results that we want and that no one will be able to get into the data and steal what they would like.

How to Create a Table

Now that we have been able to go through and create a database of our own, it is time for us to go through and create one of the tables that we are talking about here.

You will find that once the database is done and ready to go, it is pretty easy to use a simple command in SQL to create one of the tables.

You can technically add in as many of these tables to the database as you would need to help keep your information nice and safe in the process.

The syntax that you can use when it is time to work with creating the tables that you need in your new database will include:

CREATE TABLE table_name (
   column1 datatype,
   column2 datatype,
   column3 datatype,

....
);

With this one, you will find that the parameters that we have around the columns are going to help us to specify the names of the columns that we have in this kind of table.

Then we will also have the parameter for the data type that we want to work with, and this one is going to be important because it tells us the data type that we would like the column to hold.

You can choose what kind of data you would like to place here, but it would be something like a date, an integer, or varchar, for example.

How to Delete Tables

We have now taken some time to see how we can create one of the tables that we need in our database.

This is going to be useful when we need to sort through some of the data that we are using in SQL and want to make sure that it is all found in one place.

Creating these tables is pretty easy, and you can use as many of these as you would like along the way.

With this in mind, we also need to take a quick look at how we can delete some of these tables.

Over time, you may find that one of the tables that you are working with is going not to work the way that you would like, or maybe the information is outdated, and you would just like to clean it up and make it look a bit nicer without that table.

This is something that you can do with the right codes in place.

The code that you will be able to use to make it easier to delete any of the tables that you would like in your database will include:

DELETE FROM *table_name* WHERE *condition*;

One thing to remember with this is that we need to be careful at any time that we want to be able to delete a record out of a table.

We have to notice the WHERE clause as well as the DELETE statement.

The WHERE clause is there to let the compiler know which of the records in specific you would like to see deleted.

But if you do not add in this clause, you will find that all of the records of the table will be deleted.

If that was your original goal, that is not a big deal, but it can make you lose a lot of information if you are not careful about what you are doing.

Checking the Integrity of a Database

Before we end with this chapter, we need to make sure that we are checking the integrity of our SQL database.

This will ensure that the information is safe and secure and that all of the data that is coming in is going to be secure and will work the way that you would like.

There are a few reasons why you would like to make sure that you check out the integrity of this SQL database.

Some of these are going to include:

- If you find that one of the servers is running into some issues or has bugs in the environment and this is starting to go over to more than one of the servers of your SQL.
- There is the potential for some inconsistencies between the server primary and log files and the database as well.
- When you need to run some diagnostics to make sure that we are going to be able to check all of the integrity points of all the objects that are found in a specific database.

- When we want to make sure that we can remove any of the corruption of our data that could potentially cause all sorts of issues inside of the database that we are working with.
- Frequently when we end up with lots of statements in SQL that are failing, when we are not getting the results that we need that are correct, and when the instances are not working.

There are several methods that we can work with, to maintain some of the integrity that we need with our database, but you will find that it takes some time, and you need to make sure that you are maintaining the right focus on the things that are needed.

Always pay the most attention to the high priority kinds of databases, and then work your way down.

This makes sure that the information that is the most important is going to end up getting the most attention in the process.

Chapter 13: Database Administration

Once you have your database up and running with tables and queries, it is up to you to keep the production database running smoothly.

The database will have to be regularly looked at to ensure that it continues to perform as originally intended.

If a database is poorly maintained, it can easily result in a website connected to it performing poorly or worse still result in downtime or even data loss.

There is usually a person designated to look after the database, and their job is titled Database Administrator or DBA.

However, it's usually a non-DBA person who needs help with the database.

There are several different tasks which you can perform when carrying out maintenance which include the following:

Database Integrity: When you check the integrity of the database, you are running checks on the data to make sure that both the physical and logical structure of the database is consistent and accurate.

Index Reorganization: Once you start to insert and delete data on your database, there is going to be fragmentation (or scattering) of indexes.

Reorganizing the index will bring everything back together again and increase speed.

Rebuild Index: You don't have to perform an index reorganization, you can drop an index and then recreate them.

Database Backup: One of the most important tasks to perform.

There are some different ways in which you can back up the database, these include: full which backs up the database entirely, a differential which backs up the database since the last full backup, and a transaction log which only backs up the transactional log.

Check Database Statistics: You can check the statistics of the database, which are kept on queries.

If you update the statistics, which can get out of date, you can help aid the queries being run.

Data and Log File: In general, make sure the data and log files are kept separate from each other.

These files will grow when your database is being used, and it's best to allocate them an appropriate size going forward (and not just enable them to grow).

Depending on your database, some tasks may be more useful than others. Apart from a database backup, which probably is mandatory if it's in production, you can pick through the other tasks depending on the state of the database.

For example, should the fragmentation of the database be below 30%, then you can choose to perform an index reorganization.

However, if the database fragmentation is greater than 30%, then you should rebuild the index.

You can rebuild the index weekly or more often if possible. You can run a maintenance plan on SQL Server via its Server Agent depending on database requirements.

It's important to set the times right, not when your application is expected to be busy.

You can choose a time, or you can run it when the server CPU is not busy. Choosing to run when the server is not busy is a more preferred option for larger databases than selecting a particular time as there is no guaranteed time in which the CPU will be idle.

However, it is usually only a concern if your application is quite big and has a lot of requests.

When you do rebuild the indexes, you must have the results sorted in tempdb.

When using tempdb the old indexes are kept until new ones are added. Normally rebuilding the indexes uses the fixed space in which the database was allocated.

So, if you run out of disk space, then you would not be able to complete the rebuilding of indexes. It's possible to use the tempdb and not have to increase the database disk size.

The database maintenance can be run both synchronous (wait for task completion) or asynchronous (together) to speed things up; however, you should ensure the tasks are running in the right order.

Setting up a Maintenance Plan in SQL Server

To set up a maintenance plan in SQL Server, you first must get the server to show advanced options.

This is achieved through executing the code that follows in SQL Server as a new query:

sp_configure 'show advanced options', 1

GO

RECONFIGURE

GO

sp_configure 'Agent XPs', 1

GO

RECONFIGURE

GO

SQL Server will now display the advanced options.

Left-click the + icon to the left of Management, which is on the left-hand side of SQL Server Management Studio.

Now left click Maintenance Plans and then right-clicked Maintenance Plans.

Select New Maintenance Plan Wizard.

Enter an appropriate maintenance plan name and description.

From here, you can both, run one or all tasks in one plan, and have as many plans as you want.

After you have given a name, choose a single schedule, and click next.

You will see several options that you can pick for your maintenance including checking your database integrity, shrinking the database, reorganizing index, rebuilding the index, updating the statistics, clean up history, executing SQL server agent job, back-up—full, differential, or transaction log, and maintenance cleanup task.

Select which you want to perform (in this example, select all).

This wizard will bring you through each of the items you have selected to fine-tune them.

Once you select the items you want in your plan, click next, you can now rearrange them in the order you wish them to complete.

It's best to have Database Backup first in case of power failure, so select it and move it to the top of the list. Click next.

Define Back Up Database (Full) Task

This screen will give you the freedom to pick which full database backup you wish to perform it on.

The best practice is to keep one plan per database, select one database, and select next.

Define Database Check Integrity Task

This screen—the integrity task is a SQL Server command that aims at inspecting the database's integrity to see if everything is not corrupt and stable.

Select a database and click next.

Define Shrink Database Task

You can now configure shrink the database to free up space on the next screen.

It will only shrink space if available, but should you need space in the future, you will have to reallocate it.

However, this step will help backup speeds. Most developers don't use this feature that much. Click next after selecting a database to shrink.

Define Reorganize Index Task

The next screen is the Define Reorganize Index Tag screen. When you add, modify, and delete indexes, you will, like tables, need to reorganize them.

The process is the same as a hard disk where you have there are fragmented files and space scattered across the disk. The best practice is to perform this task once per week for a busy database.

You can choose to compact a large object which compacts any index which has large binary object data.

Click next to proceed to the next screen.

Define Rebuild Index Task

This part covers individual index rows. As mentioned, either reorganize or reindexing. Doing both together in one plan is pointless. Depending on your fragmentation level, pick one or the other. In this example, select your database and sort results in tempdb. Click next to proceed.

Define Update Statistics Task

The update statistics task helps the developer keep track of data retrieval as its created, modified, and deleted. You can keep the statistics up to date by performing this plan. Both statistics for index and statistics for individual columns are kept. Select your database and click next to proceed.

Define History Cleanup Task

You should now see the Define maintenance cleanup task screen, which specifies the historical data to delete.

You can specify a shorter time frame to keep the backup and recovery, agent job history, and maintenance place for on the dropdown. Click next to proceed.

Define Back up Database (Differential) Task

This screen allows you to back up every page in the database, which has been changed since the last full backup. Select a database you wish to use and click next to proceed.

Define the Backup Database (Transaction Log) Duty

The transaction log backup backs up all the log records since the last backup. You can choose a folder to store it. Performing this type of backup is the least resource-intensive backup. Select a database and storage location and click next.

Define Execute SQL Server Agent Job Task

The SQL Server Agent Job Task deals with jobs that are outside the wizard. For example, it could be to check for nulls, check whether the database meets specified standards, etc. Any jobs that are specified in SQL Server Agent Job Task are listed here.

Click next to proceed.

Define Maintenance Cleanup Task

This screen defines the clean-up action of the maintenance task i.e. to ensure that they are not taking up unnecessary space, so you can specify where to store them. You can delete specific backup files.

Click next to proceed.

Report Options

The next screen covers where you want to store the report of the maintenance plan. Make a note of where you are going to store it. You need to have an email set up on SQL Server to email it. Click next to proceed.

Complete the Wizard

The final screen is a complete review of the wizard. You can review the summary of the plan and which options were selected. Clicking finish ends the wizard and creates the plan. You should now see a success screen with the tasks completed.

Running the Maintenance Plan

Once you successfully complete the maintenance wizard, the next step is to run the plan you created. To get the plan to run, you need to have the SQL Server Agent running. It is visible 2 down from where Management is on SQL Server Management Studio. You can left-click SQL Server Agent and then right-click and select Start.

Also, you can press the Windows key + and press the letter r, then type in services.msc and hit return. Once Services appear, scroll down and look for SQL Server Agent (MSSQLEXPRESS).

You can install SQL Server Express or select the other versions like (MSSQLSERVER) if you installed that. Left-click it, then right-click it and select Start. You can go back to SSMS and right-click on the maintenance plan you created under maintenance plans and then select Execute. This will now run your plan.

On successful completion of the plan, click ok and close the dialogue box. You can view the reports by right-clicking the maintenance plan you created and selecting View history. On the left-hand side are all the different plans in SQL Server while on the right are the results of the specific plan.

Emailing the Reports

A lot of DBA's like to get their database reports via email.

What you need to do is to set up a database mail before you can fire off emails and then set up a Server agent to send the email.

Configuring the Database Mail

The first step is to right-click Database mail in SSMS and select configure database mail.

A wizard screen will appear, then click next.

Now select the first choice – set up Database Mail and click next.

Enter a profile name optional description of the profile.

Now click on the Add button to the right.

This will bring you to an add New Database Mail Account – SMTP.

You need to enter the STMP details for an email account.

Maybe you can set up a new email account for this service.

You can search online for SMTP details, Gmail works quite well (server name: smtp.gmail.com, port number 587, SSL required, tick basic authentication & confirm password).

Click on ok.

Click next, click on public (important: so it can be used by the rest of the database).

Set it as the default profile, click next, click next again.

You should now get a success screen.

Click close.

> Possible Error: It is important to ensure you select yes to public profile when you are at the Manage Profile Security part of the wizard above. If there is no public profile – no emails can be sent. You can check by running the following in a new query and check to ensure

SQL Server Agent

To send off the database email, you need to set up a Server Agent.

Start by right-clicking on SQL Server Agent–New–Operator. Give the operator a name like Maintenance Plan Operator and enter in the email address you wish to send the report to and click ok.

Now right the maintenance plan that you have successfully executed and selected modify. The maintenance plan design screen will appear on the right-hand side, where you can see some graphics of the tasks completed in it.

Now click on Reporting and Logging—it is an icon situated on the menu bar of the design plan—to the left of Manage Connections.

The Reporting and Logging window will appear. Select the tick box—Send report to an email recipient and select the Maintenance plan operator you just created.

The next time you run the plan, an email will be sent to the email address. The running and maintenance of a database is an important job.

Having the right plan for your database means it will continue to work as originally designed, and you can quickly identify database errors or slowdowns early on and fix them quickly.

Backup and Recovery

The most important task a DBA can perform is to back up the database. When you create a maintenance plan, it's important to have it top of the maintenance list in case the job doesn't get fully completed.

Firstly, it is important to understand the transaction log and why it is important.

The Transaction Log

Whenever a change is made to the database, be it a transaction or modification, it is stored in the transaction log. The transaction log is the most important file in a SQL Server database, and everything resolves around either saving it or using it.

Every transaction log can facilitate transaction recovery, recovery of all incomplete transactions, rolling forward a restored file, filegroup, or page to the point of failure, transactional replication, disaster recovery.

Recovery

The first step in backing up a database is choosing a recovery option for the database.

You can perform the 3 types of backups when SQL Server is online and even while users are making requests from the database.

Recovery Models

When you backup and restore in SQL Server, you do so in the context of the recovery model, which are models designed to control the maintenance of the transactional log. The recovery model is a database property that controls how transactions are logged.

There are 3 different recovery options: Simple, Full, and Bulk Logged.

Simple Recovery

You cannot back up the transactional log when utilizing the simple recovery model. Usually, this model is used where updates are infrequent.

Transactions are logged to a minimum, and the log will be truncated.

Full Recovery

In the full recovery model, the transaction log backup must be taken. Only when the backup process begins will the transactional log be truncated. You can recover to any point in time.

However, you also need the full chain of log files to restore the database to the nearest time possible.

Bulk Logged

This model is designed to be utilized for short term use when you use a bulk import operation. You use it along with the full recovery model whenever you don't need a certain point in time recovery.

It has performance gains and also doesn't fill up the transaction log.

Changing the Recovery Model

To change the recovery model, you can right-click on a database in SQL Server Management Studio and selecting properties, then select options, and then select the recovery mode from the drop-down box.

Or you can use one of the following 3:

ALTER DATABASE SQLEbook SET RECOVERY SIMPLE

GO

ALTER DATABASE SQLEbook SET RECOVERY FULL

GO

ALTER DATABASE SQLEbook SET RECOVERY BULK_LOGGED

GO

Backups

There are 3 types of backup: full, differential, and transaction log:

Full Backup

When you create a full backup, SQL Server creates a CHECKPOINT, which ensures that any dirty page that exists is written to disk. Then SQL Server backs up each page on the database. It then backs up the majority of the transaction log to ensure there is transactional consistency.

What all of this means is that you can restore your database to a most recent point and have all the transactions, including those right up to the very beginning of the backup.

Differential Backup

The differential backup, as its name suggests, backs up every page in the database which has since been modified since the last backup.

SQL Server keeps track of all the different pages that have been modified via flags and DIFF pages.

Transaction Log Backup

With the log backup, SQL Server backs up the data in the transaction log only, i.e. only the transactions that were recently committed to the database.

The transaction log is not as resource hungry and is considered important because it can perform backups more often without having an impact on database performance

Backup Strategy

When Database Administrator sets out a backup plan, they base their plan on 2 measures: RTO (Recovery Time Objective) and RPO (Recovery Point Objective.)

The RTO reflects the period taken to recover after notification of a disruption in the business process.

RPO measures the timeframe that might pass during a disruption before the data size that has been lost exceeds the maximum limit of the business process.

If there was an RPO of 60 minutes, you couldn't achieve this goal if the backup was set to every 24 hours.

You need to set your backup plan based on these 2 measures.

Full Backup

Exercising this alone is the least flexible option. Essentially your only able to restore your database back to one point of time, which is the last full backup. So, if the database went corrupt 2 hours from midnight (and you backup at midnight), your RPO would be 22 hours.

Also, if a user truncated a table 2 hours from midnight, you would have the same 22-hour loss of business transactions.

Full Backup and Log Backup

If you have selected Full Recovery mode, you can run both full backups and transactional log file backups. You can run more frequent backups since running Transaction Log backup takes fewer resources. This is a very good choice if your database is updated throughout the day. When you are scheduling transactional log backups, it is best to follow the RPO. Thus, if you have an RPO of 60 minutes, then set the log file backups to

60 minutes. However, you must check the RTO for such a backup.

If you had an RPO of 60 minutes and are only performing a full backup once a week, you might not be able to restore all 330 backups in the allotted time.

Full, Differential, and Log Backup

To get around the problem mentioned above, you can add differential backups to the plan.

A differential backup is cumulative, which means a serious reduction in the number of backups you would have to restore to recover your database to the point just before failure.

Performing a Backup

To back up a database, right-click the database in SSMS then select Tasks-> Backup. You can select what kind of backup (full, differential, or transaction log) to perform and when to perform a backup.

The copy-only backup allows you to perform a backup, which doesn't affect the restore sequence.

Restoring a Database

When you want to restore a database in SSMS, right-click the database, then select Tasks–Restore–Database.

You can select the database from the drop-down, and thus, the rest of the tabs will be populated. If you click on Timeline, you will see a graphical diagram of when the last backup was created, which shows how much data was lost. You can recover to the end of the log or a specific date and time.

The Verify Backup Timeline media button enables you to verify the backup media before you restore it. If you want to change where you are going to store the backup, you can click on the Files to select a different location. You can specify the restore options that you are going to use on the Options page. Either overwrite the existing database or keep it. The recovery state either brings the database online or allows further backups to be applied.

Once you click OK on the bottom, the database will be restored.

Chapter 14: Real-World Uses

Since the replacement of paper files stored in a physical file cabinet, relational databases have given way to new ground.

Relational database management systems or RDBMS, for short, are used anywhere information is stored or retrieved, like a login account for a website or articles on a blog.

Speaking of which, this also gave a new platform and helped leverage web sites like Wikipedia, Facebook, Amazon, and eBay.

Wikipedia, for instance, contains articles, links, and images, all of which are stored in a database behind-the-scenes.

Facebook holds much of the same type of information, and Amazon holds product information, payment methods, and even handles payment transactions.

With that in mind, banks also use databases for payment transactions and to manage the funds within someone's bank account.

Other industries, like retail, use databases to store product information, inventory, sales transactions, price, and so much more. Medical offices use databases to store patient information, prescription medication, appointments, etc.

To expand further upon databases, using the medical office, for example, allows for numerous users to be able to connect to the database at one time and interact with its information. Since it uses a network to manage connections, virtually anyone with access to the database can access it from just about anywhere in the world.

Since the age of the digital database, it helps leverage mobile applications and provides new opportunities for software, or any other platforms that use databases daily, to be developed.

One app that comes to mind would be an email app, as it's storing the emails on a server somewhere in a data center and allowing you to view and send emails. These types of databases have also given way to new jobs and even expanded the tasks and responsibilities of current jobs.

Those who are in finance, for instance, now can run reports on financial data; those in sales can run a report for a sales forecast and so much more! In practical situations, databases are often used by multiple users at the same time. A database that can support many users at once has a high level of concurrency.

In some situations, concurrency can lead to loss of data or the reading of non-existent data.

SQL manages these situations using transactions to control atomicity, consistency, isolation, and durability. These elements comprise the properties of transactions.

A transaction is a sequence of T-SQL statements that combine logically and complete an operation that would otherwise introduce inconsistency to a database. Atomicity is a property that acts as a container for transaction statements.

If the statement is successful, then the total transaction completes. If any part of a transaction is unable to process fully, then the entire operation fails, and all partial changes roll back to a prior state. Transactions take place once a row or page-wide lock is in place.

Locking prevents the modification of data from other users that could affect the locked object. It is akin to reserving a spot within the database to make changes.

If another user attempts to change data under lock, their process will fail, and an alert communicates that the object in question is barred and unavailable for modification.

Transforming data using transactions allows a database to move from one consistent state to a new consistent state. It's critical to understand that transactions can modify more than one database at a time.

Changing data in a primary key or foreign key field without simultaneously updating the other location, creates inconsistent data that SQL does not accept.

Transactions are a big part of changing related data from multiple table sources all at once.

Transactional transformation reinforces isolation, a property that prevents concurrent transactions from interfering with each other. If 2 simultaneous transactions take place at the same time, only one of them will be successful. Transactions are invisible until they are complete.

Whichever transaction completes first will be accepted. The new information displays upon completion of the failed transaction, and at that point, the user must decide if the updated information still requires modification. If there happened to be a power outage and the stability of the system fails, data durability would ensure that the effects of incomplete transactions "rollback."

If one transaction completes and another concurrent transaction fails to finish, the completed transaction is retained. Rollbacks are accomplished by the database engine using the transaction log to identify the previous state of data and match the data to an earlier point in time.

There are a few variations of a database lock, and various properties of locks as well. Lock properties include mode, granularity, and duration.

The easiest to define is duration, which specifies a time interval where the lock is applied. Lock modes define different types of locking, and these modes are determined based on the type of resource being locked. A shared lock allows the data to read while the row or page lock is in effect.

Exclusive locks are for performing data manipulation (DML), and they provide exclusive use of a row or page for the execution of data modification. Exclusive locks do not take place concurrently, as data is being actively modified; the page is then inaccessible to all other users regardless of permissions.

Update locks are placed on a single object and allow for the data to read while the update lock is in place. It also allows the database engine to determine if an exclusive lock is necessary once a transaction that modifies an object is committed, this is only true if no other locks are active on the object in question at the time of the update lock.

The update lock is the best of both worlds, allowing the reading of data and DML transactions to take place at the same time until the actual update is committed to the row or table. These lock types describe page-level locking, but there are other types beyond the scope of this text.

The final property of a lock, the granularity specifies to what degree a resource is unavailable. Rows are the smallest object available for locking, leaving the rest of the database available for manipulations.

Pages, indices, tables, extents, or the entire database are candidates for locking. An extent is a physical allocation of data, and the database engine will employ this lock if a table or index grows, and more disk space is needed.

Problems can arise from locks, such as lock escalation or deadlock, and we highly encourage readers to pursue a deeper understanding of how these function. It is useful to mention that

Oracle developed an extension for SQL that allows for procedural instruction using SQL syntax.

This is called PL/SQL, and as we discussed at the beginning of the book, SQL, on its own, is unable to provide procedural instruction because it is a non-procedural language.

The extension changes this and expands the capabilities of SQL. PLSQL code is used to create and modify advanced SQL concepts such as functions, stored procedures, and triggers.

Triggers allow SQL to perform specific operations when conditional instructions are defined. It is an advanced functionality of SQL and often works in conjunction with logging or alerts to notify principles or administrators when errors occur.

SQL lacks control structures, for looping, branching, and decision making, which are available in programming languages such as Java.

The Oracle Corporation developed PL/SQL to meet the needs of its database product, which includes similar functionality to other database management systems but is not limited to non-procedural operations. Previously, user-defined functions were mentioned but not defined.

T-SQL does not adequately cover the creation of user-defined functions, but using programming, it is possible to create functions that fit neatly within the same scope as system-defined functions.

A user-defined function (UDF) is a programming construct that accepts parameters, performs tasks capable of making use of system-defined parameters, and returns results successfully. UDF's are tricky because Microsoft SQL allows for stored procedures that often can accomplish the same task as a user-defined function.

Stored procedures are a batch of SQL statements that are executed in multiple ways and contain centralized data access logic. Both of these features are important when working with SQL in production environments.

Conclusion

Although it can be much to learn, SQL can be a very simple language to use in a database. By taking advantage of the necessary tools in this book, you can successfully maneuver your way throughout any database.

It is important to keep in mind that not all formulas work the same in every database, and there are different versions listed in the book. There is plenty to learn when it comes to SQL, but with the use of practice and good knowledge, you can be as successful as you decide to be in any database.

Just how the English language has many rules to be followed, the same applies to SQL. By taking the time to learn the language thoroughly, many things are achievable with the use of a database. Refer back to any of the information in this book any time you are stumped on something, you are working on.

Although it can be a complex challenge, patience and practice will help you successfully learn SQL. By remembering the basic commands and rules to SQL, you will avoid any issues that can come across most individuals that practice the use of it. It is a lot of information to take in, but instead, take it as it comes.

Go to the practical tools that you may need for whatever you are trying to achieve through the database. When presented with an obstacle or complex assignment, refer to the tools that will clear up what you need.

Take time to fully analyze what is before you while also trying to focus on one thing at a time. Keep an open and simple mind when moving forward, and you will keep any issues from becoming more complicated than they need to be. As mention, SQL can be a simple thing to learn. You just need to take the time to understand what everything fully means in-depth.

If something doesn't turn out as expected, retrace your tracks to find where you might have inappropriately added formula and some of the information. By building and maintaining successful problem-solving skills, you will not limit your success.

It Is All About Asking Good Questions

If you have made it this far, you have seen how we can use Structured Query Language to turn lifeless entries in a database into meaningful information that you or your company can use to make the tough decisions that define every business venture.

Throughout this book, I have tried to demonstrate how to write efficient but intelligent queries using real-world scenarios that showcase the methods that I have found useful and still use today.

I have tried my best to avoid the philosophical debates, technicalities, and academic jargon that plague everybody of technical knowledge to bring you by the purest and most expedient path to your unique mastery of SQL.

To the beginner: I hope you have enjoyed this journey we have taken together and that I have built a bridge for you to continue on your path to data mastery.

To those with previous experience: I hope this book has highlighted a few insights and given you a sandbox to test your ever-growing SQL toolbox.

Choosing the Right Database Occupation

Although we have focused mainly on the role of the database analyst (using your skills in query composition, composing statements, and answering everyday questions), there is plenty of demand for database designers as well.

If you have ever wondered who decides what fields will be contained in any given table, or how the tables will relate to each other, that is the job of a database designer/modeler.

www.ingramcontent.com/pod-product-compliance
Lightning Source LLC
Chambersburg PA
CBHW071359210526
45465CB00001B/164